Battles of the Spirit

Understanding Spiritual Warfare

Adelia C. Minett

Copyright © 2024 by Adelia C. Minett

All rights reserved.

No portion of this book may be reproduced in any form without written permission from the publisher or author, except as permitted by U.S. copyright law.

This publication is designed to provide accurate and authoritative information in regard to the subject matter covered. It is sold with the understanding that neither the author nor the publisher is engaged in rendering legal, investment, accounting or other professional services. While the publisher and author have used their best efforts in preparing this book, they make no representations or warranties with respect to the accuracy or completeness of the contents of this book and specifically disclaim any implied warranties of merchantability or fitness for a particular purpose. No warranty may be created or extended by sales representatives or written sales materials. The advice and strategies contained herein may not be suitable for your situation. You should consult with a professional when appropriate. Neither the publisher nor the author shall be liable for any loss of profit or any other commercial damages, including but not limited to special, incidental, consequential, personal, or other damages.

Contents

Introduction	1
1. The Unseen Battlefield: Defining Spiritual Warfare	5
2. Arming the Soul: Building Your Spiritual Arsenal	20
3. The Adversary Unmasked: Knowing Your Enemy	35
4. Strategies of Resistance: Standing Firm in Battle	50
5. The Invisible Armor: Cultivating Inner Strength	64
6. The Shadow Within: Understanding and Overcoming Inner Battles	78
7. Waging War in Prayer: Strategies for Spiritual Breakthrough	92
8. Weapons of Light: Overcoming Darkness with Divine Authority	106
9. The Role of Community in Spiritual Warfare	120
10. After the Battle: Maintaining Spiritual Victory	134
Conclusion	148

Introduction

In every culture, across every civilization, there has always been a sense of something greater. This unseen reality moves beneath the surface of our physical world. Whether acknowledged or ignored, this invisible realm is believed by many to hold immense power, influencing human thoughts, emotions, and actions in ways that often go unnoticed. This book, *Battles of the Spirit: Understanding Spiritual Warfare*, ventures into this hidden landscape, shedding light on what spiritual warfare truly is, why it happens, and how we can combat it with the strength of our spirit.

Spiritual warfare is a phrase that can stir a variety of reactions—from fear and skepticism to curiosity and reverence. Some see it as a metaphor for the inner struggles we face. In contrast, others believe it is a literal clash between supernatural forces of good and evil. Whatever the perspective, one thing is clear: when left unchecked, the battle within can wreak havoc on the mind, emotions, and even physical well-being. To understand spiritual warfare is to gain insight into these battles, to recognize them when they occur, and to develop strategies to fight back.

But what exactly is spiritual warfare? At its core, it is the clash of two opposing forces: light and darkness, truth and deceit, love and fear. This battle can manifest in various ways—through temptations, negative thoughts, emotional turmoil, and even external circumstances that seem to conspire against us. Often, it appears as an all-out assault on one's faith, hope, and purpose, leaving individuals feeling overwhelmed, confused, or paralyzed by despair. While the physical world is the stage on which we live our lives, this unseen realm shapes much of what we experience and perceive.

There is a tendency to dismiss spiritual warfare as a relic of superstitious thinking, something that belongs to an age before the modern era of science and technology. Yet, the conflicts of the soul have persisted, defying time and logic. Despite the advancements in our understanding of the mind and human behavior, many face inexplicable resistance when pursuing what they know is good or true. This resistance can take many forms—self-doubt, persistent temptations, destructive habits, or emotional burdens that seem to have no clear cause. These invisible barriers point to a deeper reality where spiritual forces are at play, subtly shaping our lives.

In *Battles of the Spirit*, we will delve into this profound concept, unraveling the complexities of the spiritual realm and exploring how to navigate through the unseen battles that affect our thoughts, behaviors, and circumstances. This journey is not about focusing solely on the negative or instilling fear but about gaining wisdom, strengthening the spirit, and empowering ourselves to stand firm in the face of adversity. For those who believe in spiritual realities, this book will serve as a roadmap for effectively engaging with these unseen forces. For others, it may offer a compelling perspective on the unexplained struggles and conflicts that surface in everyday life.

To comprehend spiritual warfare, it's essential to understand both the visible and invisible dimensions of existence. Picture life as a theater. The stage is set with visible scenery and actors—the people, places, and events that fill our days. But behind the curtain, hidden from view, there is an intricate network of unseen dynamics—the spiritual influences, unseen presences, and energies that shape the course of what unfolds on the stage.

We miss the hidden causes that move the narrative forward when we only focus on the visible. Like puppets without a puppeteer, we can end up trying to solve problems with the wrong set of tools, treating only the symptoms while ignoring the root cause.

This book aims to peel back that curtain, exposing the strategies of darkness and, more importantly, revealing the tools and weapons available for resisting and overcoming spiritual attacks. We'll start by defining spiritual warfare, examining its origins, and identifying the various manifestations it can take. The battlefield is vast and varied, from internal struggles with negative thoughts to external confrontations that disrupt our peace. The more we understand these dynamics, the better equipped we are to engage with them.

The truth is, whether we acknowledge it or not, everyone is involved in some form of spiritual warfare. The battleground may differ from person to person—one may struggle with deep-rooted fears, another with anxiety or self-sabotaging behaviors, while others may face temptations that lead them astray from their purpose. But regardless of the nature of the conflict, the war is real, and so are the weapons at our disposal.

We'll explore these weapons in detail—prayer, faith, fasting, and the power of truth, to name a few. But more importantly, we'll focus on understanding how to use them effectively. Imagine a soldier given the finest armor and weapons but no training to wield them. Without skill and strategy, these tools are nearly useless. Similarly, spiritual warfare requires more than simply knowing about faith or prayer; it involves mastering these tools with precision and persistence.

Throughout the book, we'll also address identity as a critical element of spiritual warfare. Understanding who you are and what you stand for is paramount. Often, the enemy's strategy is not just to attack your circumstances but to distort your perception of yourself—to sow seeds of doubt, fear, and confusion about your worth and purpose. By reclaiming your true identity and standing firm in it, you weaken the enemy's grip and open the door to victory.

Ultimately, *Battles of the Spirit* empowers you to confidently engage with these unseen battles. It's about equipping you with the knowledge, discernment, and strategies needed to recognize spiritual warfare when it arises and to stand firm when you are caught in its midst. By the end of this journey, you will not only be aware of the spiritual battlefield but will have the wisdom and strength to fight and overcome. This book is not a quick fix or a promise of an easy path but a call to arms for those ready to take a stand in the unseen realm, confronting darkness with the light of truth and emerging victorious.

Chapter One

The Unseen Battlefield: Defining Spiritual Warfare

When you consider the concept of spiritual warfare, it's easy to overlook the invisible forces in your daily life. You might find yourself caught in a struggle with no clear origin, yet it's rooted in a cosmic clash between good and evil. Understanding this unseen battlefield requires more than passive acknowledgment; it demands active engagement and discernment. But what happens when you begin to recognize these forces? The implications could transform your perspective entirely, leading you to explore deeper truths about your spiritual resilience.

Understanding the Invisible Realm

Many might underestimate the significance of the invisible forces in spiritual warfare. You must recognize that these forces, often dismissed as mere metaphors, constitute a fundamental aspect of Christian doctrine. The Scriptures frequently reference a spiritual sphere that interacts with our physical world, suggesting a complex interplay between divine and demonic influences.

Understanding this invisible sphere requires you to engage with key biblical texts. Ephesians 6:12, for instance, states, "For we don't wrestle against flesh and blood, but against rulers, against authorities, against cosmic powers over this present darkness, and against spiritual forces of evil." This passage highlights that your struggles aren't limited to the tangible; they extend into a sphere where spiritual entities influence human affairs.

Moreover, the concept of the unseen is pivotal in shaping your spiritual responses. It necessitates vigilance and discernment, compelling you to seek God's guidance through prayer and the study of Scripture.

The Origins of the Conflict: Cosmic Clash of Good and Evil

The conflict between good and evil finds its roots in the very fabric of creation, where the divine order established by God faced a rebellion led by Satan and his followers. This clash isn't merely an abstract idea but a foundational doctrine that shapes the understanding of spiritual warfare.

In the celestial hierarchy, God created beings with free will, which allowed for the possibility of rebellion. Satan, originally an angel of light, chose to oppose God, seeking to usurp divine authority. This decision set into motion a cosmic conflict that reverberates through time.

As you explore the origins of this spiritual warfare, consider the implications of free will. The very act of creation imbued beings with the capacity to choose between good and evil. This choice is central to understanding the ongoing battle; it reveals the nature of God as loving and just, desiring genuine relationships with His creation. However, it also exposes the profound consequences of rebellion.

The biblical narrative vividly illustrates this cosmic clash, from Lucifer's fall to humanity's temptations in the Garden of Eden. Each event underscores the reality of spiritual opposition and the necessity for vigilance.

This conflict isn't confined to ancient history; it manifests in the daily struggles of individuals seeking to align with divine truth against the backdrop of moral ambiguity. Recognizing the origins of this battle equips you to engage in spiritual warfare with clarity and purpose, understanding the stakes involved in the cosmic clash of good and evil.

Common Misconceptions and Myths

Many people grapple with misconceptions about spiritual warfare, often viewing it through a lens of fear or superstition rather than a grounded understanding of biblical doctrine. One prevalent myth is that spiritual warfare is solely about exorcisms or dramatic confrontations with evil entities. While these scenarios exist, they represent only a fraction of a broader spiritual conflict. Spiritual warfare encompasses everyday struggles against sin, temptation, and the influences that seek to undermine your faith.

Another common misconception is that spiritual warfare is something you can engage in passively. It requires active participation and engagement with the Word of God. Ephesians 6:12 teaches that your struggle isn't against flesh and blood but against spiritual forces. This highlights the need for a proactive approach, including prayer, scripture study, and community support.

Many also mistakenly believe that spiritual warfare is a battle you can fight alone. The biblical model emphasizes the importance of the Church as a collective body, reinforcing the idea that you're not meant to navigate these challenges in isolation. Community prayer, accountability, and mutual support are essential.

Lastly, the notion that victory in spiritual warfare guarantees a life free from struggles is misleading. Trials and tribulations remain part of the Christian journey. Understanding that spiritual warfare is ongoing rather than a one-time event helps you navigate faith with realism and hope. Embracing these truths can empower you for the battles ahead.

How Spiritual Warfare Manifests in Everyday Life

Spiritual warfare often manifests subtly in everyday life, revealing itself through the choices you make and the thoughts you entertain. Each day, you face myriad decisions that can either align with spiritual truths or veer into deception.

Consider how your thought patterns serve as a battleground; feelings of doubt, anxiety, or resentment can infiltrate your mind, leading you away from peace and purpose. These internal struggles often reflect a larger spiritual conflict, where your focus shifts from faith to fear.

Your interactions with others also play a significant role in this warfare. The way you communicate—whether through kindness or criticism—can create ripples that impact relationships and the community. When you extend grace rather than harbor bitterness, you engage in spiritual resistance, reinforcing a life grounded in doctrine and love.

Moreover, the media you consume can subtly shape your worldview. Engaging with content that promotes negativity or conflict can erode your spiritual armor, making you more susceptible to distractions and temptations. In contrast, immersing yourself in uplifting and doctrinally sound materials fortifies your spirit.

Ultimately, spiritual warfare isn't confined to dramatic encounters; it permeates the mundane aspects of life. You can navigate this unseen battlefield with intention by cultivating awareness of your thoughts, choices, and influences.

Each moment presents an opportunity to reaffirm your commitment to spiritual truth, enabling you to stand firm amidst the daily skirmishes that threaten your spirit.

Identifying the Adversaries: Dark Forces and Their Schemes

While navigating daily life's complexities, it's important to recognize the adversaries that seek to undermine your spiritual journey. These dark forces often act subtly, yet their schemes can profoundly affect your spiritual well-being. Understanding these adversaries' identities is significant for your defense against their influence.

Here are four primary adversaries to be aware of:

1. **Demonic Entities**: These beings, often depicted in scripture, actively work to distract, deceive, and destroy your faith. They exploit weaknesses and sow discord in your life.

2. **Worldly Influences**: The culture around you can serve as a powerful adversary. Materialism, secularism, and moral relativism can draw you away from spiritual truths, leading to a diluted faith.

3. **Internal Doubts**: Your mind can be an adversary when it harbors doubts, fears, and insecurities. These thoughts can disrupt your spiritual focus and weaken your resolve.

4. **False Teachings**: Doctrinal errors and misleading philosophies

can confuse and lead you astray. It's crucial to discern truth from falsehood to protect your spiritual integrity.

The Role of Human Will and Temptation

Recognizing the adversaries of your spiritual journey sets the stage for understanding the interplay of human will and temptation. Within this framework, your will is both a battleground and a weapon. You possess the innate ability to make choices that align with your spiritual values or to succumb to the allure of temptation, which often manifests as desires contrary to your higher self. This dynamic underscores the doctrine of free will, asserting that while external forces may influence you, the ultimate decision remains in your hands.

Temptation, often viewed as a test, seeks to exploit weaknesses in your character. Recognizing its insidious nature is essential; it doesn't always present as overtly sinful but can masquerade as seemingly benign distractions. For instance, prioritizing material gain over spiritual growth can subtly divert you from your path. Your ability to discern these subtleties is a reflection of your spiritual maturity.

Moreover, the interplay between your will and temptation can lead to a cycle of struggle. You might experience moments of resistance and failure, which can foster a sense of guilt or despair. However, these experiences can also catalyze growth, prompting you to reassess your commitments and strengthen your resolve.

Self-reflection and seeking guidance through prayer or meditation can empower you to exercise your will more effectively. Ultimately, understanding this interplay equips you to navigate the complexities of spiritual warfare with greater clarity and purpose.

Spiritual Warfare in Religious Texts: Interpretations Across Faiths

Various religious writings interpret the concept of warfare in multifaceted ways, revealing deep-seated beliefs about the human condition and the divine struggle against evil.

You'll notice that different faiths articulate spiritual warfare in ways that reflect their unique theological frameworks. This understanding can help you appreciate the complexity and richness of these narratives.

1. **Christianity**: The New Covenant emphasizes the armor of God (Ephesians 6:10-18), portraying believers as engaged in a battle against spiritual forces of darkness, highlighting the necessity of divine protection and faith.

2. **Islam**: The concept of jihad, often misunderstood, encompasses an inner struggle against sin and an external struggle for justice, underscoring the importance of intention and righteousness in spiritual combat.

3. **Judaism**: Writings like the Book of Psalms depict spiritual warfare as a plea for divine intervention against adversaries, illustrating the belief in God's active role in the fight against evil.

4. **Hinduism**: The Bhagavad Gita presents the concept of dharma, where spiritual warfare is framed as a moral duty. It emphasizes the internal conflict of righteous action versus personal desires.

Misalignment of Perception: Are You Ignoring the Battle?

Many individuals overlook the ongoing spiritual battle that manifests both internally and externally, often due to a misalignment of perception. This misalignment stems from a lack of awareness regarding the spiritual dimensions of their lives, which can lead to significant consequences.

You may focus solely on the physical sphere of your daily routine. At the same time, the true struggle unfolds in the spiritual domain. The scriptures emphasize that our battle isn't against flesh and blood but against spiritual forces (Ephesians 6:12). This notion invites you to reevaluate your perspective.

Your perception of reality shapes your understanding of spiritual warfare. When you ignore the signs of conflict—such as feelings of anxiety, despair, or moral confusion—you risk falling prey to spiritual complacency. Doctrine teaches that these feelings often signify a deeper, unseen battle. By failing to recognize this, you might inadvertently fortify the strategies of opposition forces, allowing them to influence your thoughts and actions.

Moreover, spiritual alignment is essential. Engaging in regular spiritual practices—prayer, scripture study, and community worship—reinforces your awareness of the battle. When you neglect these practices, you create a gap in your defenses.

In this state of misalignment, you may become susceptible to deception, misinterpreting your experiences and dismissing the reality of spiritual warfare. Acknowledging this battle is the first step toward empowerment and discernment, enabling you to navigate the spiritual landscape with clarity and purpose.

Recognizing Spiritual Oppression and Its Impact

Spiritual oppression often manifests as a heavy burden on the mind and soul, subtly influencing your thoughts, emotions, and actions. Recognizing its signs is important for spiritual clarity and emotional well-being. This oppressive state can stem from various sources, including unresolved sin, negative influences, or external spiritual attacks.

It's imperative to identify the symptoms to engage effectively in spiritual warfare.

Consider these indicators of spiritual oppression:

1. **Persistent Hopelessness**: You may find yourself engulfed in despair, feeling as if there's no light at the end of the tunnel.

2. **Emotional Volatility**: Sudden mood swings or overwhelming anger can signal an external spiritual influence disrupting your peace.

3. **Loss of Interest**: Activities that once brought joy may seem meaningless, reflecting a disconnect from your spiritual energy.

4. **Isolation**: A desire to withdraw from community and fellowship can indicate an oppressive force trying to sever your connections.

These symptoms can hinder spiritual growth and distort one's perception of God's love and purpose in life. Acknowledging these signs is the first step toward liberation.

You can combat this oppression by engaging in prayer, seeking counsel, and immersing yourself in scripture. It's crucial to remember that spiritual warfare involves recognizing the enemy's tactics and actively seeking God's strength and guidance to reclaim your spiritual freedom.

Understanding these dynamics allows you to navigate the unseen battlefield with discernment and resilience.

When Spiritual Conflicts Turn Psychological

Conflict often emerges when spiritual battles seep into psychological territories, complicating your mental and emotional landscape. This interplay between the spiritual and psychological domains can create a vortex of distress that distorts your perception of reality and self. When you're engaged in spiritual warfare, the pressures and influences may manifest not only as spiritual struggles but also as psychological turmoil, blurring the lines between faith-based challenges and mental health issues.

In this context, it's vital to recognize that spiritual conflicts can lead to cognitive dissonance. You may wrestle with doubts about your beliefs, prompting anxiety or depression. The scriptures emphasize the importance of renewing the mind (Romans 12:2). Yet, you might find yourself entrenched in fear or confusion, exacerbating feelings of isolation or hopelessness.

Moreover, spiritual warfare can engender feelings of inadequacy, leading to a negative self-image that can spiral into deeper psychological issues. The enemy often exploits these vulnerabilities, turning your spiritual battles into a psychological battleground where guilt and shame thrive. Recognizing this dynamic is essential for spiritual resilience.

Addressing your struggles holistically—acknowledging both the spiritual and psychological dimensions—enables you to seek appropriate support through prayer, counseling, or community engagement. Doing so can reclaim your mental and emotional well-being while remaining steadfast in your spiritual journey.

Is It All in Your Mind? The Mental Battle

The interplay between psychological struggles and spiritual warfare often leads to profound questions about the nature of your mental battles. You might wonder if these conflicts are merely products of your mind or if they reflect deeper spiritual realities. Understanding this duality is essential for maneuvering through your experiences effectively.

Here are four key aspects to reflect on:

1. **Cognitive Dissonance**: You may experience a conflict between your beliefs and actions, creating inner turmoil. This dissonance can manifest as doubt, fear, or confusion, clouding your spiritual clarity.

2. **Emotional Warfare**: Your emotions can serve as battlegrounds. Feelings of anxiety, anger, or despair can distract you from spiritual truths, making it necessary to recognize these emotions as potential tools of spiritual deception.

3. **The Role of the Mind**: Scripture emphasizes the importance of your thoughts (Philippians 4:8). By focusing your mind on positive spiritual truths, you can combat negative thought patterns that hinder your spiritual growth.

4. **Spiritual Discernment**: It's important to distinguish between psychological struggles and spiritual attacks. Developing discernment helps you identify the source of your battles, guiding you toward appropriate responses in prayer and action.

In essence, your mental battles aren't solely psychological; they often have spiritual underpinnings. Recognizing this interplay empowers you to engage more effectively in your mental and spiritual journeys, allowing for holistic growth and healing.

The Consequences of Spiritual Ignorance

Ignoring spiritual truths can lead to dire consequences in your life. When you neglect the principles of spiritual warfare, you risk becoming vulnerable to influences that exploit your ignorance. Scripture warns against this ignorance, as it often leads to deception and a weakened faith. Without a solid understanding of spiritual realities, you may find yourself ill-equipped to discern truth and falsehood, leaving you susceptible to manipulative ideologies and emotional turmoil.

Moreover, spiritual ignorance can result in a lack of discernment in your relationships and decision-making processes. When you fail to recognize the spiritual dimensions of your interactions, you may unwittingly align yourself with negative influences that undermine your values and convictions. This misalignment can lead to destructive patterns in personal relationships or broader societal contexts.

Additionally, the consequences of spiritual ignorance extend beyond individual experiences. They can manifest in collective spiritual apathy, where communities become disengaged from their foundational beliefs. This detachment can foster an environment ripe for moral decline and societal chaos, undermining the very essence of communal faith.

It's crucial to actively pursue knowledge of spiritual truths to combat these consequences. Engaging with doctrine, participating in community discussions, and seeking guidance through prayer and study can fortify one's understanding.

Can Unseen Battles Affect Physical Reality?

Spiritual ignorance leaves individuals vulnerable to deception and obscures the reality of unseen battles that directly influence physical outcomes.

These battles aren't just abstract concepts; they manifest in ways that affect your daily life, relationships, and overall well-being. Recognizing this connection is essential for understanding the intricate dynamics between spiritual warfare and physical reality.

Consider the following ways unseen battles can impact your life:

1. **Emotional Distress**: Unseen spiritual forces can manipulate emotions, leading to anxiety, fear, or depression. These feelings can profoundly affect your decision-making and interactions.

2. **Physical Health**: Chronic stress or spiritual oppression may manifest as physical ailments. The mind-body connection is powerful, and spiritual battles can improve your health.

3. **Relationship Strain**: Spiritual conflicts often spill over into interpersonal relationships. Division, strife, and misunderstandings can arise due to unseen influences affecting your connections with others.

4. **Life Direction**: Spiritual warfare can derail your purpose and calling. When you're engaged in unseen battles, you may find yourself distracted or confused about your path in life.

Why Awareness is the First Step to Victory

While many may underestimate the significance of awareness in spiritual warfare, acknowledging its presence is vital for achieving victory. Awareness is the foundation for spiritual discernment, enabling you to recognize the subtle influences that can affect your thoughts, emotions, and decisions. This discernment is essential, as it allows you to differentiate between divine guidance and deceptive distractions that can lead you astray.

When you cultivate awareness, you actively engage with the spiritual dimension, becoming attuned to the dynamics around you. This heightened perception allows you to identify the enemy's tactics, whether they manifest as temptation, doubt, or spiritual lethargy. By recognizing these influences, you gain the power to counteract them, employing the armor of faith and the Word of God as your defense.

Moreover, awareness promotes a proactive approach to spiritual warfare. Instead of reacting to challenges as they arise, you can anticipate potential spiritual pitfalls and prepare yourself accordingly. This preparation involves regular self-reflection, prayer, and scripture study, reinforcing your understanding of the spiritual landscape and fostering resilience against attacks.

In essence, awareness isn't merely about recognizing external threats but understanding your internal landscape. By fostering awareness, you position yourself to respond effectively to the unseen battles that seek to undermine your spiritual growth.

Ultimately, this awareness paves the way for a more victorious and fulfilling Christian life, empowering you to stand firmly against the forces that oppose you.

The Spiritual Warrior's Mindset: Preparation and Perspective

Cultivating awareness naturally leads to developing the mindset of a spiritual warrior, where preparation and perspective become essential.

You must understand that your mindset is your greatest asset to engage effectively in spiritual warfare. This involves being aware of the battles around you and preparing yourself spiritually and mentally.

Here are four key elements to evaluate in shaping your mindset:

1. **Daily Prayer and Meditation**: Establish a routine that deepens your connection with the divine. Prayer and meditation provide clarity, peace, and strength, which are crucial for facing spiritual challenges.

2. **Scriptural Knowledge**: Familiarize yourself with spiritual texts and doctrines. Understanding the principles of your faith equips you to combat misconceptions and reinforces your resolve.

3. **Community Support**: Surround yourself with like-minded individuals who share your beliefs. Engaging in discussions and communal worship fosters a sense of belonging and strengthens your spiritual resilience.

4. **Self-Reflection**: Regularly examine your thoughts, emotions, and actions. This practice allows you to identify areas of weakness and helps you realign your focus on spiritual growth.

Chapter Two

Arming the Soul: Building Your Spiritual Arsenal

When it comes to maneuvering the complexities of life, you might find yourself in a battle that's not just physical but deeply spiritual. Understanding your spiritual weapons—like prayer, fasting, and faith—can provide you with the resilience needed to confront challenges head-on. Each tool in your spiritual arsenal plays an essential role in shielding you against negativity and despair. As you consider how to arm your soul, the question remains: Are you prepared to engage in this profound struggle for clarity and purpose?

Understanding Your Spiritual Weapons

At the core of every spiritual journey lies a powerful arsenal of weapons designed to uplift and protect you. These spiritual weapons aren't physical tools but rather profound insights and practices that can enhance your resilience and clarity in life's challenges. Understanding these weapons is essential for your personal growth and spiritual empowerment.

First, consider mindfulness. By cultivating awareness of your thoughts and emotions, you create a shield against negativity. When you're present, you can discern between what serves your highest good and what doesn't. This clarity allows you to navigate through confusion and fear with grace.

Next, embrace gratitude. It's a transformative weapon that shifts your focus from lack to abundance. When you actively acknowledge the blessings in your life, you elevate your spirit and open yourself to even more positivity. Gratitude helps you combat despair and cultivate a sense of joy.

Additionally, practicing self-compassion enables you to face your flaws and mistakes without harsh judgment. This self-acceptance fosters a nurturing environment for growth, allowing you to rise stronger from setbacks.

Finally, connect with your intuition. Trusting your inner voice guides you through uncertainty, acting as a compass during turbulent times. By honing this skill, you empower yourself to make choices aligned with your true purpose.

Understanding your spiritual weapons is about recognizing the inner strengths and practices that can fortify your spirit. Equip yourself with these tools, and watch as you transform challenges into opportunities for growth and enlightenment.

The Power of Prayer: A Shield and Sword

Prayer is one of the most powerful tools in your spiritual arsenal. It acts as a shield against adversity and a sword that cuts through doubt. When you pray, you're not merely reciting words but entering into a dynamic conversation with the divine. This connection fortifies your spirit, allowing you to face challenges with courage and clarity.

Here are three key aspects of prayer that empower you in your spiritual battles:

1. **Protection**: When you pray, you invoke a divine presence surrounding you with peace and strength. This shield helps deflect negativity and fear, enabling you to stand firm in life's storms.

2. **Clarity**: Prayer helps clear mental fog and confusion. By seeking guidance through prayer, you align your thoughts with higher wisdom, making it easier to discern the right path and decisions in difficult situations.

3. **Strength**: Each time you pray, you build spiritual muscle. Just as physical exercise strengthens your body, consistent prayer deepens your faith and resilience, equipping you to confront doubts and trials with unwavering confidence.

In moments of doubt or despair, remember that your prayers aren't just requests; they're declarations of faith. Each prayer is a step towards empowerment, reinforcing your spirit as you navigate the complexities of life.

Embrace this power and let it transform your battles into victories.

Fasting: A Discipline to Strengthen the Spirit

Fasting can be a transformative practice that strengthens your spirit and deepens your connection to the divine. When you choose to fast, you're not just abstaining from food; you're engaging in a profound act of discipline that helps clear your mind and focus your heart. This intentional physical nourishment withdrawal opens space for spiritual growth and reflection.

During a fast, you may find that your senses heighten and your awareness of the divine presence around you intensifies. As you turn your attention away from earthly distractions, you cultivate a deeper understanding of your spiritual needs. You might uncover habits or thoughts that weigh you down, inviting you to examine them honestly. This process can bring about a renewed sense of purpose and clarity.

Fasting also teaches you to rely on God's strength rather than your own. Each moment of hunger can remind you to seek spiritual sustenance, drawing you into prayer and meditation. Replacing physical cravings with spiritual ones builds resilience and fortitude, essential traits for any spiritual warrior.

As you begin this journey, remember that fasting isn't about punishment or deprivation but liberation and growth. Embrace it as a sacred opportunity to align your spirit with divine intent.

Through fasting, you'll discover the power of self-discipline and the richness of your relationship with the divine, fortifying you for the battles that lie ahead.

The Role of Faith: Belief as Your First Line of Defense

Faith serves as the unwavering foundation upon which your spiritual journey is built, acting as your first defense against life's challenges.

It's the beacon guiding you through storms, reminding you that you're not alone in your struggles. When you cultivate a strong belief, you equip yourself to face adversity with courage and resilience.

Here are three crucial aspects of faith that bolster your defenses:

1. **Trust**: Embracing faith means relying on something greater than

yourself. This trust creates a safety net, allowing you to surrender your fears and uncertainties, knowing that every trial has a purpose.

2. **Hope**: Faith instills a sense of hope that illuminates your path, even in the darkest moments. It whispers promises of better days ahead, encouraging you to keep moving despite obstacles.

3. **Community**: Your faith connects you to others who share similar beliefs. Surrounding yourself with a supportive community fosters strength and accountability, reminding you that together, you can face any challenge that comes your way.

The Armor of God: Biblical Strategies for Protection

When you suit up in the Armor of God, you're not just preparing for battle but embracing a powerful toolkit designed to shield you from life's spiritual attacks.

Each piece of this divine armor serves an essential purpose, empowering you to stand firm against negativity and doubt.

The belt of truth holds everything together, reminding you to be honest not just about the world around you but also about who you are in God's eyes.

The breastplate of righteousness protects your heart, ensuring that your intentions are pure and your actions reflect your faith.

As you lace up your shoes of peace, you prepare to walk confidently in every situation, spreading hope and calmness wherever you go.

And when the fiery darts of fear and temptation come your way, the shield of faith is your first line of defense, extinguishing those flames with unwavering trust in God's promises.

You're not alone in this struggle; the helmet of salvation guards your mind, allowing you to think with clarity and purpose, while the sword of the Spirit equips you with God's Word, cutting through confusion and lies.

Psalms and Scriptures: Word as a Weapon

As you wield the Scriptures in your daily life, you uncover a powerful weapon that can transform your circumstances and uplift your spirit. The Psalms and other sacred texts are a direct line to divine strength, providing comfort and guidance during battles.

When you immerse yourself in the Word, you're not just reading; you're arming your soul with resilience.

Here are three essential ways Scriptures act as your weapon:

1. **Affirmation of Truth**: In moments of doubt or fear, the verses remind you of your identity and purpose. They affirm that you're loved, worthy, and never alone—powerful truths that combat the enemy's lies.

2. **Encouragement in Trials**: Life's challenges can feel overwhelming, but the Psalms reveal the heart of God amidst adversity. They encourage perseverance, instill hope, and remind us that joy comes in the morning.

3. **Prayer and Declaration**: When you declare the Word over your life, you engage in spiritual warfare. These verses become your battle cries, invoking divine intervention and protection as you

navigate the storms of life.

Embrace the Scriptures as your sword, using them to pierce through negativity and despair.

Each verse you memorize and meditate on equips you for the daily skirmishes of life, empowering you to stand firm in faith.

Personal Sanctification: Building a Stronghold of Purity

Building a stronghold of purity in your life is crucial for personal sanctification. This process isn't just about avoiding temptation; it's about cultivating a heart and mind aligned with your highest values. Committing to purity establishes a firm foundation to navigate life's challenges with grace and strength.

Start by examining your thoughts and intentions. Reflect on what fills your mind daily—are they uplifting and pure? Surround yourself with influences that inspire holiness: uplifting books, encouraging conversations, and environments that foster growth. Remember, purity begins within; it's a matter of the heart before it manifests in actions.

Next, set boundaries that protect your spirit. Identify areas where you're most vulnerable and create safeguards. These boundaries aren't limitations; they empower choices affirming your commitment to sanctification. Whether choosing your entertainment wisely or avoiding toxic relationships, each decision fortifies your stronghold.

It's also essential to engage in regular self-reflection and prayer. Take time to assess your journey and seek guidance. Ask for the strength to resist distractions and stay focused on your spiritual goals. As you cultivate a lifestyle of purity, you'll find clarity and purpose flowing into your life, transforming your battles into opportunities for growth.

Building this stronghold is a daily endeavor, but as you persist, you'll discover an inner resilience that equips you for spiritual warfare. Your commitment to purity will sanctify you and inspire those around you.

Harnessing the Strength of Praise and Worship

Praise and worship serve as powerful conduits for spiritual strength, connecting you with the divine while fortifying your faith. When you engage in these practices, you create an atmosphere where the spirit can thrive and become more attuned to divine guidance. It's not just about the songs you sing or the words you say; it's about the heart behind the actions.

Consider these three essential benefits of harnessing the strength of praise and worship in your life:

1. **Transformative Power**: As you lift your voice in praise, you invite transformation. Your worries, fears, and doubts fade, replaced by a sense of purpose and peace that can only come from the divine.

2. **Strengthened Connection**: Worshiping deepens your relationship with God. It's a moment of intimacy where you can express gratitude, seek guidance, and find solace, helping you navigate life's challenges with a renewed spirit.

3. **Spiritual Armor**: Praise acts as your shield in moments of spiritual battle. It's a declaration of faith that fortifies you against negativity and despair, reminding you of the blessings and promises surrounding you.

Incorporating praise and worship into your daily routine isn't just beneficial; it's essential. Make it a priority, and watch how it transforms your spiritual landscape.

Your battles may be fierce, but with praise and worship as your weapons, you'll find the strength to overcome.

Intercession: The Art of Fighting for Others

Intercession isn't just a practice; it's a profound act of love and commitment that allows you to fight for others in the spiritual domain. When interceding, you enter the gap for those struggling, lost, or needing divine intervention. It's a demonstration of your faith and a reflection of the power of community. You're not just praying but engaging in a spiritual battle for your loved ones, friends, or even strangers.

Think about the impact of your intercessory prayers. You're wielding the authority given to you, standing firm against the forces that seek to undermine those you care about. Each prayer becomes a shield, a lifeline, a beacon of hope. Imagine the transformations that can occur when you pray fervently to lift someone up, believing God hears and responds.

As you develop this practice, remember that intercession requires commitment and compassion. It's not merely about asking for help; it's about understanding others' struggles and calling upon divine strength to uplift them. You become a vessel of grace, channeling love and support through your prayers.

In the journey of intercession, your spirit will be fortified. Each time you advocate for someone else, you deepen your connection to the divine, reinforcing your faith.

Identifying Weaknesses in Your Spiritual Armor

Every believer has a unique spiritual armor, but sometimes, it can feel worn or even compromised. Recognizing these weaknesses is essential for growth and resilience.

It's time for some honest reflection. Ask yourself: where might the enemy find a chink in your armor?

Here are three common areas to reflect on:

1. **Doubt**: When you allow uncertainty to creep in, it can erode your faith. Doubt acts like rust, slowly weakening your protective layer. Challenge those thoughts with Scripture and prayer, reinforcing your trust in God's promises.

2. **Isolation**: Going it alone can leave you vulnerable. Just as a soldier thrives within a unit, you need community. Seek fellowship with other believers who can encourage and uplift you. Remember, iron sharpens iron.

3. **Neglect of Prayer**: Prayer is your lifeline. When you skip this important practice, you risk disconnecting from your source of strength. Make time each day to commune with God, fostering a relationship that fortifies your spirit.

Identifying these weaknesses isn't a sign of failure; it's an opportunity for growth. By addressing these areas, you can rebuild and reinforce your spiritual armor.

Embrace the journey of self-discovery, knowing that each step you take brings you closer to a more resilient faith. In this battle of the spirit, awareness is your first line of defense. Strengthen your armor, and stand firm!

Cultivating Resilience Through Spiritual Habits

Amid life's daily challenges, cultivating resilience through spiritual habits can transform your faith into a steadfast fortress. When you intentionally engage in practices like prayer, meditation, or scripture reading, you're not just filling your time but fortifying your spirit against the storms that inevitably arise. These habits serve as anchors, grounding you in truth when uncertainty seeks to sway you.

Start by establishing a routine that nurtures your soul. Dedicate time each day to connecting with your inner self and your Creator. Journaling your thoughts and prayers might allow you to process emotions and gain clarity. Reflecting on your experiences will reveal patterns and insights that empower your journey.

Remember, resilience isn't about avoiding hardship; it's about navigating it gracefully. Spiritual habits help you develop this capacity, enabling you to respond to challenges with a calm and focused mindset. When you're rooted in your faith, you cultivate a perspective that sees setbacks as opportunities for growth rather than insurmountable obstacles.

Surround yourself with a community that uplifts and encourages you. Engaging in fellowship provides support and accountability, reminding you you're not alone in your struggles. You can build each other up together, fostering resilience that flourishes in unity.

Ultimately, by committing to these spiritual habits, you're not just surviving life's battles but thriving through them, emerging stronger and more grounded in your faith. Embrace this journey, and watch your resilience blossom.

Developing Discernment: Knowing When to Act

Discernment acts as a compass, guiding you through the complexities of life and helping you know when to take action. In a world filled with distractions and uncertainties, it's crucial to hone this skill to navigate your spiritual journey effectively.

You'll find that discernment isn't just about making decisions; it's about recognizing the right moment to act.

To develop your discernment, consider these three key practices:

1. **Pause and Reflect**: Before acting, take a moment to breathe and assess the situation. This allows you to distance yourself from impulsive reactions and opens up space for clarity.

2. **Seek Wisdom**: Surround yourself with individuals who inspire and challenge you spiritually. Their insights can provide a different perspective and help you weigh your options more thoughtfully.

3. **Trust Your Intuition**: Your inner voice often knows more than you realize. Tune into your feelings and instincts; they can guide you toward the right course of action.

The Role of the Holy Spirit in Battle

Harnessing the power of the Holy Spirit in spiritual battles can transform your struggles into victories. You're not alone in this fight; the Holy Spirit is your divine ally, guiding and empowering you through every challenge. When you invite His presence into your battles, you tap into a strength that surpasses human understanding.

The Holy Spirit brings clarity to your mind, enabling you to discern the true nature of your struggles. He whispers reassurance in moments of doubt or fear, reminding you of God's promises and your inherent worth. This divine guidance helps you confidently navigate the complexities of life's spiritual warfare.

Moreover, the Holy Spirit equips you with essential spiritual gifts for battle. Whether it's wisdom, faith, or discernment, each gift is a tool in your spiritual arsenal, empowering you to face obstacles head-on. You'll find that these gifts strengthen you and encourage those around you, creating a ripple effect of hope and resilience.

As you pray and worship, the Holy Spirit ignites your passion and fervor, reigniting your spirit and fortifying your resolve. He empowers you to stand firm, reminding you that victory isn't merely a destination but a journey of faith and reliance on God.

Embrace the Holy Spirit's role in your battles. Lean on His strength, listen to His voice, and watch your spiritual landscape transform, turning trials into triumphs.

Focusing on Truth: Deflecting Deception and Lies

Truth is your greatest ally on the spiritual battlefield, serving as a shield against the myriad of deceptions and lies that seek to undermine your faith. When you anchor yourself in truth, you're not just defending yourself but also empowering your spirit to rise above confusion and fear.

Lies can be incredibly subtle, creeping into your thoughts and distorting your perception of reality.

To effectively focus on truth, consider these three essential practices:

1. **Daily Reflection**: Spend time each day meditating on spiritual truths. This could be through scripture, prayer, or quiet contemplation. Allow these truths to saturate your mind and heart, grounding your faith.

2. **Community Support**: Surround yourself with like-minded individuals who uplift you with their commitment to truth. Engage in discussions that reinforce clarity and encourage accountability. Remember, you're not alone in this battle.

3. **Discernment Training**: Cultivate the ability to discern between truth and deception. This involves actively questioning thoughts in your mind and comparing them to established truths. Ask yourself, "Does this align with what I know to be true?"

The Importance of Consistency and Vigilance

Consistency and vigilance are essential companions on the path to deeper understanding and growth in your spiritual journey. They empower you to stay grounded, especially amidst life's distractions and challenges. When you commit to regular practices—whether prayer, meditation, or study—you create a rhythm that nurtures your spirit and fortifies your resolve against spiritual battles.

Consistency isn't just about routine; it's about establishing a foundation that allows you to thrive. By dedicating time to reflecting on and reconnecting with your beliefs, you reinforce your values and principles. This foundation becomes your refuge, your armor in times of doubt or temptation.

You'll find that the more you engage with your spiritual practices, the stronger your intuition and discernment will become. This will aid you in recognizing the subtle deceptions that seek to derail your progress.

Vigilance complements this consistency. It's about being aware of the influences around you and guarding your heart against negativity and distractions. Life can often lead you astray, but by remaining vigilant, you cultivate the strength to resist these forces.

Pay attention to your thoughts, feelings, and actions; they reveal your spiritual state.

Consistency and vigilance create a powerful synergy. They deepen your spiritual experience and empower you to stand firm in your beliefs. By embodying these qualities, you'll navigate your spiritual journey with purpose, resilience, and an unwavering connection to your higher self.

Chapter Three

The Adversary Unmasked: Knowing Your Enemy

You might think you know the enemy you face in spiritual battles, but the reality is often more complex. Each tactic employed—deception, division, or despair—can manifest in ways that challenge your faith and purpose. Understanding the deeper structures of evil and its strategies can fortify your defenses against these subtle yet powerful forces. But what do these dark influences look like, and how can you distinguish between genuine guidance and misleading spirits? The answers may reshape your approach to resilience and strength in the face of adversity.

The Anatomy of Evil: Understanding the Dark Forces

To explore the anatomy of evil, one must first recognize that it exists within and around us, shaping our perceptions and actions. This duality of existence invites you to confront the uncomfortable truth that evil isn't merely an external force; it often resides in your choices and the motivations that drive you. By examining evil's nature, you gain insight into its manifestations, ranging from subtle manipulations to overt acts of malice.

Evil often thrives in the shadows, obscured by rationalizations and societal norms. However slight, you may justify harmful actions, believing they serve a greater purpose. This cognitive dissonance becomes a breeding ground for moral decay as you begin normalizing behaviors you once deemed unacceptable. Acknowledging these tendencies is essential; self-reflection is your first line of defense against the encroachment of darkness.

Moreover, you're confronted with the idea that evil can be systemic, permeating institutions and cultures. Recognizing this allows you to see how collective actions can perpetuate harm, often under the guise of tradition or authority. By understanding these dynamics, you empower yourself to challenge these systems and promote justice.

Ultimately, grappling with the anatomy of evil requires confronting one's own biases, fears, and capacities for harm. This self-awareness fortifies one's spirit and equips one to engage in the ongoing struggle against the dark forces that threaten to undermine one's moral compass.

Principalities, Powers, and Spiritual Wickedness

Recognizing the existence of evil within and around you naturally leads to exploring the spiritual hierarchies that influence human behavior—principalities, powers, and spiritual wickedness. These terms, often derived from biblical texts, encapsulate different domains of spiritual influence.

Principalities are overarching authorities or rulers, often presiding over specific geographical or cultural territories. They assert control in ways that can manifest through societal norms, governmental structures, or even ideologies that steer collective human action.

On the other hand, Powers represent the mechanisms of influence and manipulation at a more localized level. They operate within the frameworks established by principalities, enabling the execution of wills through subjugation, coercion, or seduction. You might observe their daily effects on individuals' pervasive temptations or moral compromises. These powers thrive in environments where ethical boundaries blur, leading to a culture of compliance and fear.

Spiritual wickedness, the most insidious of the three, embodies the essence of malevolence. It acts in shadows, exploiting vulnerabilities and fostering despair through deceit and hopelessness.

Understanding these hierarchies is essential when engaging in spiritual warfare. Recognizing their existence and mechanisms allows you to identify the influences at work and the world around you. You gain the insight needed to counteract these forces, enabling you to fortify your spirit against their pervasive reach.

Satan's Strategies: Deception, Division, and Despair

Three primary strategies define Satan's approach to spiritual warfare: deception, division, and despair. Each strategy undermines your faith and disrupts your relationship with God and others. Understanding these tactics can empower you to resist and counteract their effects.

Deception is perhaps the most insidious of Satan's methods. He often disguises lies as truths, leading you to question your beliefs and the integrity of God's Word. By distorting reality, he creates confusion, blurring the lines between right and wrong. This tactic can sow seeds of doubt in your mind, making you vulnerable to further manipulation.

It's essential to remain anchored in Scripture and rely on the Holy Spirit for discernment.

Next, the division seeks to fracture your relationships with fellow believers and within your family. When you allow bitterness, jealousy, or pride to take root, you become susceptible to Satan's influence. He thrives on discord, exploiting misunderstandings and creating rifts.

To combat this, nurture unity and practice forgiveness, recognizing that these actions counteract the enemy's schemes.

Demonic Influence vs. Possession: Key Differences

Demonic influence and possession represent two distinct manifestations of spiritual warfare, each with unique implications for a believer's life. Understanding these differences is vital for recognizing how they can affect your spiritual journey.

Demonic influence occurs when malevolent forces tempt, manipulate, or sow confusion in one's thoughts and actions. This influence can manifest through negative emotions, destructive behaviors, or doubts about one's faith. It's a constant battle against external pressures that can lead one away from God's truth.

In contrast, possession is a much more severe condition where a demon takes control of an individual's body and mind. This possession can strip a person of their free will, often leading to drastic changes in behavior, speech, or consciousness.

It's important to note that possession typically occurs in individuals who've opened themselves up to such spiritual attacks, often through practices contrary to Christian teachings.

While both situations involve demonic activity, the key difference lies in the level of control exerted. In influence, you maintain your autonomy, although your choices may be clouded by temptation.

With possession, that autonomy is severely compromised, leading to a struggle that can manifest in extreme ways. Recognizing these distinctions empowers you to take appropriate spiritual actions, whether engaging in prayer and scripture to combat influence or seeking deliverance for more severe possession cases.

Understanding these nuances equips you for the spiritual battles you may face, ensuring you remain vigilant in your faith.

Subtle Attacks: How Darkness Masquerades as Light

Identifying subtle attacks in spiritual warfare requires discernment, as darkness often disguises itself as light. You may find that the most insidious forms of spiritual conflict don't come with overt malevolence but rather appear as benign influences that gradually lead you away from the truth. This masquerade can manifest through distorted perceptions of morality, where what seems virtuous is, in fact, a veiled deception.

Consider how societal norms can shape your understanding of good and evil. The allure of popular beliefs may entice you to accept ideas that conflict with your core values. This pressure can create a cognitive dissonance, causing you to doubt your convictions. You might rationalize behaviors or beliefs that, on the surface, seem harmless but ultimately dilute your spiritual integrity.

Moreover, emotional appeals can be particularly deceptive. Feelings of compassion, empathy, or even anger may cloud your judgment, leading you to support causes misaligned with your spiritual principles. You risk becoming a pawn in a larger, darker agenda when you act based on these emotions without critical examination.

In traversing this landscape, it's crucial to cultivate a practice of reflection and prayer. Engaging with scripture and seeking community wisdom can sharpen your discernment.

The Weapons of the Enemy: Fear, Doubt, and Isolation

In spiritual warfare, fear, doubt, and isolation are powerful weapons that the enemy uses to undermine one's faith and resilience.

These tactics are insidious, infiltrating your mind and spirit when you least expect it. Fear can paralyze you, robbing you of the courage to take action or make decisions aligned with your beliefs. When you allow fear to take root, it distorts your perception and leads you away from the truth.

Doubt is corrosive, eroding your confidence in God's promises. The nagging voice questions your worthiness, urging you to reconsider your faith. When you entertain doubt, you create a chasm between you and faith's assurance.

Isolation is perhaps the most dangerous of these weapons. It separates you from the community and support you need, fostering a sense of loneliness that amplifies fear and doubt. When you feel isolated, you become more susceptible to negative thoughts and feelings, making it easier for the enemy to manipulate your mindset.

To combat these weapons effectively, consider the following:

- **Recognize Fear**: Acknowledge fear when it surfaces; don't let it dictate your choices.

- **Challenge Doubts**: Confront your doubts with truth and reaffirm your faith.

- **Seek Community**: Surround yourself with supportive individuals who uplift and encourage you.

Understanding these weapons enables you to fortify your spirit and reclaim your strength in the face of spiritual battles.

Recognizing the Signs of Spiritual Attacks

Recognizing spiritual attacks can be challenging, especially when fear, doubt, and isolation cloud your judgment. Yet, developing the ability to identify these signs is essential for your spiritual resilience.

One of the primary indicators of a spiritual attack is a sudden onset of negative emotions. You might find yourself overwhelmed by feelings of despair, anxiety, or anger that seem disproportionate to your circumstances. These emotions can obscure your sense of peace and disrupt your daily life.

Another sign to be aware of is persistent confusion or doubt regarding your beliefs and values. This isn't just a momentary questioning; it's a deep-rooted uncertainty that can lead you to second-guess your faith or purpose.

Pay attention to patterns of self-sabotage, such as procrastination or a lack of motivation to engage in activities that once brought you joy.

Isolation is also a significant indicator. If you notice a tendency to withdraw from friends, family, or community, this could signal an attempt by spiritual forces to separate you from support systems. This isolation often amplifies feelings of fear and inadequacy.

Lastly, be mindful of any unexplained physical symptoms, such as fatigue or illness, which can sometimes manifest as a result of spiritual duress.

Recognizing these signs allows you to confront the attacks effectively. By staying vigilant and grounded in your faith, you can better navigate these challenges and reclaim your spiritual energy.

The Role of Curses, Hexes, and Spells

Curses, hexes, and spells represent a significant aspect of spiritual warfare, often wielded by those seeking to exert control or influence over others. While you may find it unsettling to contemplate how these tools can disrupt lives and relationships, understanding their role in spiritual dynamics allows you to navigate these challenges more effectively.

These elements of spiritual warfare share common themes, often rooted in intention and belief. When someone casts a curse or hex, they typically channel negative energy, hoping to bring harm or misfortune. Spells may vary in purpose, but they often aim to manifest specific outcomes, for better or worse. Recognizing these distinctions can help you discern the nature of the attacks you face.

- Curses can create a binding effect, limiting a person's potential or freedom.

- Hexes often aim to bring misfortune, sowing discord in relationships or endeavors.

- Spells may serve as tools for manipulation, influencing thoughts or actions.

As you reflect on the implications of curses, hexes, and spells, contemplate the broader context of spiritual warfare. These practices underscore the reality of a spiritual battle, where unseen forces seek to disrupt your peace and purpose.

Breaking Generational Strongholds

Generational strongholds can considerably impact one's life, often manifesting as recurring patterns of behavior or beliefs that stem from familial influences. These strongholds can create a cycle of negativity, shaping one's decisions, relationships, and self-perception.

To effectively confront and break these strongholds, it's vital to first recognize their presence in your life. Awareness is the first step toward liberation, allowing you to distinguish inherited patterns from your authentic self.

Reflect on the narratives passed down in your family. Do you notice themes of fear, inadequacy, or failure? These narratives often serve as a blueprint, influencing your choices and limiting your potential.

Analyzing how these beliefs align or clash with your current values and aspirations is important. You may find that some of these inherited beliefs don't serve your growth.

Once you've identified these strongholds, you can begin to dismantle them. This process often involves intentional prayer, seeking wisdom, and self-reflection.

Surrounding yourself with a supportive community can also provide encouragement as you navigate this challenging journey.

Remember, breaking generational strongholds isn't just about rejecting the past; it's about redefining your identity and embracing a healthier narrative.

In doing so, you create space for healing and transformation. By challenging these entrenched beliefs, you free yourself and pave the way for future generations to break free from similar patterns.

Understanding and addressing generational strongholds can lead to profound spiritual and personal growth.

Combatting Personal Demons: Addictions and Obsessions

Personal demons, often manifesting as addictions and obsessions, can create significant barriers to spiritual and emotional well-being. These challenges affect your day-to-day life and can cloud your spiritual journey.

When you find yourself caught in a cycle of addiction or fixation, it's vital to recognize the underlying motivations and triggers that drive these behaviors. Understanding your personal demons allows you to confront them directly, paving the way for healing and growth.

To combat these demons effectively, consider the following:

- **Self-awareness**: It is essential to cultivate an understanding of your thoughts and feelings. Reflect on when cravings arise and what emotions accompany them.

- **Support systems**: Engaging with friends, family, or support groups can provide the accountability and encouragement you need to overcome these challenges. You don't have to fight alone.

- **Spiritual practices**: Incorporating prayer, meditation, or other spiritual disciplines into your daily routine can fortify your resolve. These practices can help you reconnect with your higher self and foster resilience against temptations.

Recognizing that addictions and obsessions are often rooted in deeper spiritual conflicts empowers you to take action.

Embrace this journey of self-discovery and healing. By identifying and addressing your personal demons, you can reclaim your spiritual path and achieve a more profound sense of peace and fulfillment.

The Use of Symbolism in Spiritual Warfare

Symbolism is essential in spiritual warfare, serving as a powerful tool for understanding and combating unseen forces. Recognizing and employing symbols can amplify your awareness and intention when you engage in spiritual battles. These symbols often represent deeper truths, guiding you toward a more profound understanding of your spiritual environment. For instance, the cross may symbolize victory over sin, while light often represents divine guidance amidst darkness.

In your spiritual practice, you might find that certain symbols resonate with your specific struggles. This resonance can create a tangible connection to the spiritual domain, allowing you to focus your intent and energy more effectively. Additionally, these symbols can serve as reminders of your identity and purpose, reinforcing your resolve against adversarial influences.

Understanding the historical and cultural context of these symbols enriches their significance. Many symbols have been used for centuries, embodying collective wisdom and shared experiences that transcend individual battles. By tapping into this collective consciousness, you empower yourself with a rich legacy of spiritual warfare.

Furthermore, visualizing these symbols during prayer or meditation can enhance your spiritual defenses. Concentrating on these representations cultivates an inner strength that can fortify your spirit against negative influences.

Ultimately, symbolism in spiritual warfare isn't merely about recognition; it's about harnessing these powerful tools to effectively navigate the complexities of unseen battles.

Can Evil Spirits Latch onto Objects?

The question of whether evil spirits can latch onto objects is profound, prompting both spiritual inquiry and psychological reflection. Many believe that inanimate objects can become conduits for malevolent forces, serving as vessels for energy or intention. This belief isn't merely superstition; it reflects deeper truths about human experience and the interplay between the physical and spiritual domains.

When you consider this phenomenon, it's vital to reflect on the following points:

- **Historical Context**: Throughout history, various cultures have recognized the potential for objects to harbor spiritual energy, often attributing curses or blessings to them.

- **Psychological Attachment**: Your emotional connections to certain items may amplify their significance, making them more susceptible to negative influences.

- **Intentionality**: The energy you invest in an object through love or fear can impact its spiritual resonance and the potential for external entities to interact with it.

Understanding that objects can carry spiritual weight allows you to approach your environment with greater awareness.

Whether it's a cherished heirloom or an everyday item, evaluating the energy surrounding these objects could reveal insights into your spiritual health.

It's important to maintain vigilance and discernment, as the potential for evil spirits to latch onto objects isn't just an abstract concept—it's a real possibility that invites you to cultivate a protective mindset.

This awareness can empower you in your journey through spiritual warfare.

The Role of Angels and Protectors in Combat

As you navigate the complexities of spiritual warfare, recognizing the presence and influence of angels and protectors becomes paramount. These spiritual beings serve as divine sentinels to aid you in your battles against unseen adversaries. Their roles aren't merely symbolic; they actively engage in the spiritual domain, providing guidance, support, and, when necessary, intervention.

Angels, as messengers of the divine, possess unique attributes that empower them in combat. Their unwavering loyalty and commitment to their mission enable them to counteract malevolent forces. Knowing that angels can bolster your resolve and shield you from spiritual harm, you might find solace. Their presence often instills a sense of peace, reminding you that you aren't alone in your struggles.

Protectors, whether they manifest as guardian angels or other spiritual allies, serve to fortify your defenses. They're attuned to your vulnerabilities and can help you develop strategies to withstand spiritual assaults. By fostering a relationship with these protectors, you cultivate an environment of resilience and strength.

It's essential to remain open to their guidance through prayer, meditation, or conscious reflection. Engaging in these practices can deepen your awareness of their influence, allowing you to harness their support effectively.

Ultimately, understanding the role of angels and protectors in combat enriches your spiritual journey and equips you with the tools necessary to confront the challenges ahead.

Discerning False Prophets and Spirits of Confusion

Steering through the spiritual landscape requires a keen eye to discern false prophets and spirits of confusion that can lead you astray. In a world filled with competing messages, developing a discerning spirit is essential. False prophets often present themselves as messengers of light, yet their teachings can deviate markedly from established truths. These individuals may exploit your trust and vulnerability, steering you away from your intended spiritual path.

To sharpen your discernment, consider the following key indicators:

- **Consistency with Scripture**: Always measure teachings against sacred texts. If they contradict foundational truths, they warrant scrutiny.

- **Fruit of the Spirit**: Observe the character and outcomes of those delivering messages. Genuine prophets exhibit love, joy, peace, and other fruits of the Spirit.

- **Community Wisdom**: Engage with a trusted spiritual community. Collective discernment often uncovers blind spots in individual understanding.

In honing your ability to discern, you're actively participating in spiritual warfare. The stakes are high; misinformation can sow seeds of doubt and confusion in your heart.

By fostering a critical mindset, you empower yourself against deceptive influences. Remember, discernment isn't merely about rejecting falsehood; it's about embracing a deeper, enriched understanding of truth.

As you navigate your spiritual journey, remain vigilant and open, seeking wisdom and clarity. Your ability to discern protects you and enhances your spiritual growth, enabling you to thrive amidst the challenges of spiritual warfare.

The Endgame of the Enemy: Derailment of Purpose

While steering your spiritual journey, it's crucial to recognize that the enemy's ultimate aim often revolves around derailing your purpose. This derailment manifests in various forms, including doubt, distraction, and despair. The adversary understands your unique calling and will employ cunning tactics to exploit your weaknesses, often targeting your confidence and resolve.

One of the primary strategies involves instilling doubt about your abilities and worthiness. When you start questioning your purpose, you become vulnerable to the enemy's influence, leading to stagnation or abandonment of your spiritual mission.

Distraction is another potent tool; the enemy bombards you with trivial pursuits that pull you away from your true calling, leaving you spiritually depleted and directionless.

Moreover, despair can creep in as a subtle but effective means of derailment. When faced with challenges, the enemy may amplify your fears, convincing you that your efforts are futile. This emotional turmoil can cause a disconnect from your spiritual foundation, making it increasingly difficult to reclaim your focus and purpose.

To counter these tactics, it's crucial to cultivate awareness of your spiritual goals and remain steadfast in your convictions. Establishing a prayer, reflection, and community support routine can fortify you against the adversary's strategies.

Ultimately, understanding the enemy's endgame equips you to navigate the complexities of spiritual warfare, ensuring that you stay aligned with your divine purpose and fulfill your calling with clarity and conviction.

Chapter Four

Strategies of Resistance: Standing Firm in Battle

Understanding the tactics of resistance is essential in your journey through spiritual warfare. You might find that setting up spiritual boundaries and daily prayer can greatly influence your resilience. The spoken word holds power, yet the quiet moments of reflection often reveal deeper truths. As you navigate these complexities, consider how to actively fortify your spirit against adversarial forces. What strategies have you overlooked that could be critical in your ongoing battle?

Understanding the Tactics of Resistance

When you face resistance in your spiritual journey, you must recognize the tactics that often come against you. The enemy wants to sow doubt in your mind, whispering lies that you're not good enough or that God isn't listening. Remember the words in 1 Peter 5:8, which tell you to be alert and of sober mind. The adversary prowls around like a roaring lion, seeking to devour you. Recognizing this is your first step in standing firm.

One tactic is distraction. Life's busyness can easily draw your attention away from prayer and scripture. When you neglect your spiritual disciplines, you leave yourself vulnerable. Instead, commit to daily worship and reflection, grounding yourself in God's truth.

Another tactic is discouragement. You may feel overwhelmed by past failures or current struggles. But Philippians 4:13 reminds you that you can do everything through Christ, who strengthens you. Each setback is an opportunity to lean deeper into God's grace.

Setting Up Spiritual Boundaries

Setting spiritual boundaries is essential for maintaining your focus and strength in your faith journey. These boundaries help you guard your heart and mind against distractions and negativity.

Remember, Proverbs 4:23 encourages you to "guard your heart above all else, for it determines the course of your life." Establishing clear boundaries creates a safe space for your spiritual growth.

Here are some practical steps to set up your spiritual boundaries:

- **Prioritize Prayer**: Make daily prayer a non-negotiable part of your routine. This connection with God strengthens your resolve.

- **Limit Negative Influences**: Identify people or media that drain your spirit and set limits on your interactions with them.

- **Create a Sacred Space**: Designate a physical area in your home for prayer, meditation, or study. This space should feel peaceful and conducive to spiritual growth.

- **Set Time for Reflection**: Schedule regular moments of solitude to reflect on your spiritual journey. Journaling can be a powerful tool for this.

- **Know Your Triggers**: Be aware of situations that lead you away from your faith. When you recognize these, you can proactively avoid them.

The Power of Rebuke and Renunciation

Regularly exercising the power of rebuke and renunciation can drastically change your spiritual landscape. When confronting negativity and falsehood in your life, you tap into a divine authority that Jesus modeled throughout His ministry.

Remember, in Luke 10:19, He said, "I have given you authority... to overcome all the power of the enemy." This isn't just a promise; it's an invitation for you to act.

Rebuke isn't about anger; it's a firm declaration against the forces that attempt to sway you from your path. When you sense doubt or fear creeping in, speak against it. Say aloud, "I rebuke the spirit of fear in Jesus' name!" When you declare this, you establish a boundary, taking back control over your thoughts and emotions.

Renunciation complements rebuke, allowing you to sever ties with the spirits that have influenced you. It's about saying, "I renounce any agreement I've made with negativity." This act of faith isn't just symbolic; it's transformative.

Galatians 5:1 reminds us that "it is for freedom that Christ has set us free." Embrace that freedom by letting go of binding agreements.

As you practice these powerful tools, you'll notice a shift. Your spirit will feel lighter and your faith stronger. You're not just surviving spiritual battles but actively engaged in victory, standing firm against the enemy's tactics.

Claiming Victory Through Spoken Word

Having established the power of rebuke and renunciation, it's time to recognize the profound impact of your spoken words in claiming victory over spiritual battles. Your words carry weight; they can build, break, uplift, or tear down. When you declare God's promises, you activate His power.

Remember, the Bible tells us in Proverbs 18:21, "Death and life are in the power of the tongue." This means you have the authority to speak life into your circumstances.

Here are some practical ways to harness the power of your spoken word:

- **Declare Scripture Daily**: Speak verses that resonate with your battles, like Isaiah 54:17, proclaiming that no weapon formed against you will prosper.

- **Practice Affirmations**: Create personalized affirmations that reflect your identity in Christ, emphasizing who and who you are.

- **Pray Aloud**: Vocalize your prayers, inviting God's presence into your situation and reinforcing your faith.

- **Encourage Others**: Use your words to uplift those around you; encouragement can create a ripple effect of strength and hope.

- **Stay Thankful**: Regularly express gratitude; thankfulness shifts your focus from struggle to victory.

Deconstructing Strongholds of the Mind

Many believers unknowingly wrestle with strongholds in their minds that hinder their spiritual growth and victory. These strongholds, often built on lies, fear, or past experiences, can keep you from fully embracing the truth of God's Word.

2 Corinthians 10:4 reminds us, "The weapons we fight with aren't the weapons of the world. On the contrary, they've divine power to demolish strongholds." It's time to take action and deconstruct these barriers.

Start by identifying the specific thoughts or beliefs that don't align with God's truth. Ask yourself, "What lies am I believing?" Write them down. Once you have clarity, counter those thoughts with Scripture. For instance, if you struggle with unworthiness, remind yourself of Ephesians 2:10, which declares you're God's masterpiece.

Next, pray for God's strength to help you dismantle these strongholds. Philippians 4:6-7 encourages you to present your requests to God, promising peace in exchange for your anxiety. As you lean into prayer, your focus shifts from the stronghold to God's promises.

Lastly, surround yourself with a community of believers who can encourage and uplift you. Share your struggles and victories, and let their faith bolster your own.

Staying Grounded in Spiritual Reality

Breaking down strongholds is just the beginning of your journey toward spiritual freedom. You must stay grounded in spiritual reality to truly thrive in this newfound space. This means anchoring yourself in the truth of God's Word and recognizing your authority as a believer.

The battles you face aren't just physical; they're spiritual, and staying connected to your faith is essential.

Here are some practical strategies to help you maintain that grounding:

- **Pray Daily**: Cultivate a habit of prayer. It's your direct line to God, helping you discern His will and strength.

- **Meditate on Scripture**: Fill your mind with the truths of the Bible. Verses like Ephesians 6:10-18 remind you of your spiritual armor.

- **Surround Yourself with Community**: Engage with fellow believers. Their support and wisdom can uplift and encourage you.

- **Practice Gratitude**: Regularly reflect on your blessings. Thankfulness shifts your perspective from fear to faith.

- **Stay Alert**: Be aware of the spiritual dynamics around you. 1 Peter 5:8 calls you to be sober and vigilant against the enemy.

How to Overcome Fear During Spiritual Assaults

Fear can feel like a heavy cloak during spiritual assaults, wrapping around you and obscuring the truth of God's promises. In these moments, it's essential to remember that God hasn't given you a spirit of fear but of power, love, and a sound mind (2 Timothy 1:7).

To overcome fear, ground yourself in Scripture. When anxiety strikes, recite verses like Psalm 34:4, which assures you that the Lord delivers you from all fears.

Next, focus on worship. Singing praises shifts your perspective and invites God's presence into your situation. As you lift your voice, remember that God inhabits the praises of His people (Psalm 22:3). This act of worship can break the chains of fear and fill you with peace.

Surround yourself with a community of faith. Share your struggles with trusted friends or mentors who can pray with you and remind you of God's faithfulness.

Ecclesiastes 4:9 tells us that two are better than one, for they have a good reward for their labor.

Prayers of Protection and Deliverance

Praying for protection and deliverance can be a powerful weapon when facing spiritual battles.

These prayers shield you from negativity and invite divine help in overcoming the challenges you encounter. Remember, your words hold power, and when spoken in faith, they can shift the atmosphere around you.

Here are some effective prayers you can incorporate into your spiritual arsenal:

- **Prayer for Protection**: "Lord, I ask for your divine shield to surround me. Protect me from any harm and negativity that seeks to invade my spirit."

- **Prayer for Deliverance**: "Heavenly Father, I call upon your mighty name to deliver me from any chains that bind me. Set me free from the struggles that weigh me down."

- **Prayer for Strength**: "God, grant me the strength to stand firm in my faith. Help me resist temptation and remain steadfast in your truth."

- **Prayer for Guidance**: "Father, guide my steps as I navigate these challenges. Illuminate my path with your wisdom and clarity."

- **Prayer of Praise**: "I will praise you, Lord, for you're my refuge and strength. Your love endures forever, and I trust in your promises."

Incorporating these prayers into your daily routine can fortify your spirit and provide the protection you seek.

The Role of Community in Spiritual Warfare

In the journey of spiritual warfare, the community acts as a vital support system, amplifying your strength and resolve. Having fellow believers around you can make all the difference when you face spiritual battles. Ecclesiastes 4:9-10 reminds us that "two are better than one because they have a good reward for their labor. For if they fall, one will lift up his companion."

Your community provides encouragement, wisdom, and prayer, fortifying your defenses against spiritual attacks. Surrounding yourself with like-minded individuals means you're not alone in your struggles. When you share your burdens, you invite others to intercede on your behalf, reinforcing the power of collective prayer.

James 5:16 says, "The prayer of a righteous person is powerful and effective." With unified faith, you can stand firm, binding the enemy's schemes.

Moreover, the community fosters accountability. It's easy to waver in times of trial, but your brothers and sisters can gently guide you back to the truth. As Proverbs 27:17 states, "Iron sharpens iron, and one man sharpens another."

This sharpening process cultivates resilience and clarity as you navigate the spiritual landscape.

Prophetic Acts: Declaring Your Territory

Declaring your territory through prophetic acts empowers you to stand against spiritual opposition. When you actively engage in these acts, you affirm God's promises and claim the ground He's given you.

Prophetic acts are tangible expressions of faith that can shift the atmosphere around you and reinforce your boundaries against the adversary's schemes.

Here are some practical ways you can declare your territory:

- **Pray Over Your Space**: Walk through your home or workplace and pray specifically for each room, inviting God's presence to dwell there.

- **Use Scripture**: Write down key verses that resonate with your situation and place them in visible spots to remind you of God's truth.

- **Anoint with Oil**: Anoint doorways and windows with oil, symbolizing protection and the sealing of God's promises over your territory.

- **Create a Declaration**: Write a personal declaration that outlines what you believe God is doing in your life and read it aloud daily.

- **Worship and Praise**: Play worship music or sing praises in your space, creating an atmosphere where God's presence can thrive.

These acts aren't just rituals; they're powerful declarations of faith.

Remember, as you stand firm, God's Word promises that "no weapon formed against you'll prosper" (Isaiah 54:17).

Responding to Accusations from the Adversary

As you stand firm in your territory, the adversary will undoubtedly try to undermine your confidence through accusations and lies. When these moments arise, remember that your identity is anchored in Christ. Scripture reminds you in Romans 8:1, "There is thus now no condemnation for those who are in Christ Jesus." This powerful truth serves as your shield against the enemy's darts.

Responding to accusations requires you to first recognize their origin. The adversary aims to sow doubt and fear, but you're equipped with the Word of God. When you face accusations, counter them with truth. Speak verses out loud that affirm your worth and purpose, like Psalm 139:14, which declares, "I praise you because I'm fearfully and wonderfully made." Let these truths resonate in your spirit.

Moreover, approach accusations with prayer. Ask the Holy Spirit for guidance and clarity. In moments of uncertainty, He'll remind you of your standing in God's grace. Instead of engaging in self-defeating thoughts, declare your victory in Christ.

Finally, surround yourself with a community of believers. Share your struggles, and let their encouragement bolster your resolve. As Ecclesiastes 4:12 states, "A cord of three strands isn't quickly broken."

Embrace your identity, wield the truth, and stand firm. The battle may be fierce, but remember, you're not fighting for victory; you're fighting for victory. The adversary's accusations hold no power over you.

Removing Sources of Spiritual Contamination

A clean heart and mind are essential for thriving in spiritual warfare. To effectively combat the enemy, you must remove any sources of spiritual contamination that might hinder your progress. The enemy seeks to distract and distort your thoughts, but with God's guidance, you can cleanse your spirit and focus on His truth.

Start by identifying the influences in your life that might drag you down. Ask yourself:

- Are there relationships that negatively impact your faith?

- Is the media you consume uplifting or detrimental?

- Do you find yourself dwelling on negative thoughts or fears?

- Are you holding onto grudges or unforgiveness?

- Is your environment conducive to spiritual growth?

Once you've pinpointed these sources, take action. The Bible encourages us in 2 Corinthians 6:17, "Therefore come out from them and be separate," meaning it's crucial to distance yourself from anything that doesn't align with God's purpose for you.

Replace negative influences with uplifting ones. Surround yourself with people who encourage your faith, engage with uplifting media, and immerse yourself in Scripture.

The Role of Peace and Silence in Battle

After clearing away distractions and negative influences, you may find that peace and silence become powerful allies in your spiritual battles. In the stillness, you can connect deeply with God, allowing His voice to guide you. Scripture reminds us, "Be still, and know that I'm God" (Psalm 46:10).

This stillness isn't just the absence of noise; it's an active engagement with divine presence.

When you embrace peace, you create a sanctuary for your spirit. In these quiet moments, you can discern truth from lies and wisdom from chaos. Jesus often withdrew to solitary places to pray (Luke 5:16), demonstrating the importance of silence in seeking strength and clarity. You, too, can find rejuvenation in these moments of solitude.

Practically, carve out intentional time for silence in your daily routine. Permit yourself to be still through meditation, prayer, or simply sitting in nature.

Use this time to reflect on God's Word, allowing it to wash over you and fill you with hope. As you cultivate peace, your worries fade, replaced by a confident assurance in God's plan.

Overcoming Night Terrors and Spiritual Nightmares

Night terrors and spiritual nightmares can feel like relentless shadows stalking your peace, but you don't have to face them alone. God equips you with tools to fight back and reclaim your nights.

Remember, 2 Timothy 1:7 says, "For God hasn't given us a spirit of fear, but of power and of love and of a sound mind." Lean into that promise when you feel the grip of fear tightening.

Here are some practical strategies to help you overcome those haunting experiences:

- **Pray with intention**: Before sleep, pray specifically against fear, asking God to guard your heart and mind.

- **Scripture verses**: Memorize verses like Psalm 91:5-6, reminding yourself that you need not fear the terror of the night.

- **Create a peaceful environment**: Surround yourself with calming elements—soft lighting, soothing scents, or your favorite worship music.

- **Establish a bedtime routine**: Wind down with a routine focusing on relaxation and connection with God, like reading the Bible or journaling.

- **Seek support**: Share your struggles with trusted friends or a spiritual mentor who can pray for and encourage you.

Maintaining a Defensive Position Post-Victory

Victory in spiritual warfare is a powerful moment, but remaining vigilant and maintaining your defensive position is crucial. Just because you've won a battle doesn't mean the war is over. As Peter warns, the enemy prowls around like a roaring lion, seeking someone to devour (1 Peter 5:8). This calls for a proactive stance—don't let your guard down.

First, reinforce your defenses through prayer and scripture. Ephesians 6:17 reminds you to take the sword of the Spirit, the Word of God. Immerse yourself in the Bible, and let it be your guide and shield. Memorizing verses can be your first defense against lingering doubts or fears.

Next, stay connected to your faith community. Hebrews 10:24-25 emphasizes the importance of gathering together for encouragement and support. Surrounding yourself with fellow believers can strengthen your resolve. They can lift you up in prayer and provide the accountability you need to remain steadfast.

Additionally, cultivate a heart of gratitude. Thankfulness can disarm the enemy's tactics of discouragement. When you focus on God's goodness and past victories, you build a fortress against negativity.

Chapter Five

The Invisible Armor: Cultivating Inner Strength

You might not realize it, but the daily battles often extend beyond the physical domain, challenging your spirit profoundly. Cultivating inner strength acts as your invisible armor, equipping you to confront these unseen conflicts with resilience. By engaging in practices like meditation and mindfulness, you can transform doubt into clarity and negativity into hope. Yet, the journey to mastering this inner fortitude isn't straightforward. What strategies might truly elevate your spirit and shield you from emotional turmoil? The answers may lie in exploring the depths of your own psyche.

The Art of Meditation for Spiritual Focus

Often, the chaos of daily life overwhelms people, making it challenging to connect with their inner selves. Meditation can be a powerful tool for cultivating spiritual focus in these moments. It's not just about sitting quietly; it's about creating a sacred space within you where clarity and peace can flourish.

Start by setting aside just a few minutes each day. Find a comfortable spot, close your eyes, and take a deep breath. Allow the world's weight to melt away as you focus on your breathing. With each inhale, visualize drawing in positive energy, and with each exhale, let go of tension and distractions. This simple practice can ground you, reminding you of your strength and purpose.

As you become more familiar with meditation, you may find your thoughts wandering. That's perfectly okay! Acknowledge those distractions without judgment, and gently guide your attention back to your breath.

Over time, you'll discover that this process enhances your spiritual awareness, enabling you to connect more profoundly with your inner self.

Purifying the Mind: Thoughts as Your First Battlefield

As you cultivate your inner strength through meditation, it's important to recognize that your mind is where the real battle begins. Your thoughts can either uplift or drag you down, creating a battlefield that shapes your reality. When you allow negativity or fear to take root, it clouds your clarity and weakens your resolve.

Begin purifying your mind by consciously choosing thoughts that align with your highest self. Start by observing your thoughts without judgment. Are they supportive or critical? Acknowledge any negativity and gently redirect your focus to affirming statements. Replace "I can't" with "I can," and "What if I fail?" with "What if I succeed?" This shift isn't just about positive thinking—it's about reclaiming your power.

Utilize your meditation practice to create mental space. Visualize each thought as a leaf floating down a stream; let it pass by without clinging to it. This mindfulness fosters resilience, allowing you to confront challenges with a clearer perspective.

Dealing with Doubt: Recognizing Internal Warfare

Doubt can frequently creep into your mind, undermining your confidence and creating an internal battlefield that feels impossible to navigate. You might find yourself questioning your abilities, decisions, or even your worth.

It's crucial to recognize that this doubt isn't just a fleeting thought; it's a form of internal warfare that can sap your energy and distract you from your goals.

When you acknowledge your doubts, you take the first step toward reclaiming your inner strength. Start by identifying the specific thoughts that trigger your feelings of uncertainty. Are they rooted in past experiences, comparisons with others, or fear of failure? Naming these doubts can help demystify them, allowing you to confront them head-on.

Remember, feeling uncertain is okay; it's a natural part of the human experience.

Next, challenge those doubts. Ask yourself if they're based on facts or mere assumptions. Often, you'll find that the negative narratives you tell yourself don't hold up under scrutiny. Replace them with affirmations of your strengths and past successes. Surround yourself with supportive voices that uplift you, reminding you that you're capable and deserving of your aspirations.

Ultimately, dealing with doubt is about cultivating resilience. Recognizing it as internal warfare empowers you to fight back with clarity and confidence.

Embrace the struggle; in these moments of doubt, you often find the most profound growth. Keep pushing forward, knowing you can overcome this internal conflict.

Guarding the Heart Against Emotional Attacks

After grappling with doubt, you might feel vulnerable to emotional attacks that can further undermine your confidence.

Recognizing these feelings as part of your journey, not as a reflection of your worth, is crucial. Emotional attacks can come from various sources—harsh words from others, internal criticism, or even societal pressures. To guard your heart, start by establishing boundaries. Identify the people and situations that drain your energy or provoke negativity. It's okay to distance yourself from those influences.

Next, practice self-compassion. When you feel the sting of an emotional attack, remember that everyone experiences pain and vulnerability. Speak to yourself gently and with understanding, as you would to a friend. Acknowledge your feelings without judgment, allowing yourself the space to process them.

Additionally, cultivate a support network. Surround yourself with those who uplift and encourage you. Share your experiences with trusted friends or family members who can provide perspective and reassurance. Their support can act as a buffer against emotional onslaughts.

Cultivating Patience in Prolonged Battles

Cultivating patience is essential for maneuvering prolonged battles in the midst of life's challenges. You might feel like the world's weight is pressing down on you, and it's easy to become frustrated when things don't change as quickly as you'd like. In these moments, remember that patience isn't just about waiting; it's about maintaining a positive attitude while you navigate the storm.

Start by acknowledging your feelings. It's okay to feel overwhelmed or anxious. Instead of fighting those emotions, embrace them. Accepting your feelings can help you gain clarity and perspective on your situation.

Focus on small, manageable steps you can take each day, rather than the entire journey ahead. This shift in mindset allows you to celebrate minor victories, which can greatly boost your morale.

Mindfulness practices, such as meditation or deep breathing, can help cultivate patience. These techniques ground you in the present, reminding you that healing and resolution take time.

Surround yourself with supportive people who understand your struggles; their encouragement can be a lifeline during trying times.

Lastly, remember that every battle you face is a chance to grow stronger. Each moment of patience you cultivate builds resilience and prepares you for future challenges.

Trust that, with time and perseverance, you'll emerge from this battle with newfound strength and wisdom. Remember, you're not alone in this journey, and you're equipped with the invisible armor of patience.

How Faith Overcomes Fatigue and Weariness

Faith can be a powerful antidote to the fatigue and weariness that life often brings. When you're feeling drained, it's easy to lose sight of hope and purpose. But remember, faith isn't just a fleeting feeling; it's an anchor that can ground you during turbulent times. It reminds you that there's a greater plan at work, even when you can't see it.

When you face insurmountable challenges, let your faith be your guiding light. It can infuse your spirit with energy, helping you rise above the exhaustion that threatens to overwhelm you. Think about all the moments when you felt supported by something bigger than yourself. Those experiences can serve as a reservoir of strength, empowering you to push through weariness.

Try to incorporate small practices that nurture your faith. Whether prayer, meditation or simply reflecting on your blessings, these moments can rejuvenate your spirit and remind you that you're not alone in your struggles. Instead of succumbing to fatigue, lean into your faith. It can transform your perspective, turning obstacles into opportunities for growth.

Ultimately, faith encourages resilience. It whispers to you that every battle faced can lead to personal evolution. So, when weariness knocks at your door, embrace your faith. Let it lift you and carry you through the toughest days, reminding you that strength lies in your muscles and spirit.

Forgiveness: The Unexpected Armor of Peace

Embracing forgiveness can feel like lifting a heavy weight off your shoulders, granting you a newfound sense of peace. It's not just about letting go of anger or resentment; it's about reclaiming your joy and inner strength.

When you choose to forgive, you're not condoning someone's actions but freeing yourself from the bitterness that can bind your spirit.

You might think forgiveness is a sign of weakness, but it's one of the bravest things you can do. It takes courage to confront the hurt and decide to move forward.

By forgiving, you're taking control of your narrative and refusing to let past wounds dictate your present.

Consider the emotional toll that grudges can take. They can weigh you down, manifesting as stress or anxiety.

When you forgive, you change how you feel about others; you also change how you feel about yourself. You create space for healing, allowing love and compassion to flourish in your heart.

Remember, forgiveness is a process. It mightn't happen overnight, and that's okay.

Be gentle with yourself as you navigate this journey. Each step you take towards forgiveness is a step towards peace, and you deserve that peace.

Standing Your Ground in the Face of Opposition

Forgiveness can empower you, but standing your ground when faced with opposition is equally essential for cultivating inner strength. It's critical to hold onto your beliefs and values when challenges arise, whether from external sources or your own doubts. You might feel pressured to conform or back down but remember, your conviction is crucial to who you are.

When you encounter opposition, take a moment to breathe and center yourself. Acknowledge your feelings—fear, frustration, or even anger—without judgment. These emotions are valid, and recognizing them allows you to respond instead of react. Stand firm in your beliefs, and don't hesitate to articulate your thoughts clearly and confidently. You have the right to express your perspective, which can inspire others to do the same.

It's also important to surround yourself with a supportive community. Seek out those who uplift you and share your values. Their encouragement can fortify your resolve when you're feeling uncertain. Remember, standing your ground doesn't mean being combative; rather, it's about asserting your truth calmly and respectfully, demonstrating strength without hostility.

As you navigate these challenges, remind yourself that you're reinforcing your inner strength every time you stand firm. Each confrontation becomes an opportunity for growth. So, embrace the discomfort, stand tall, and trust that your resilience will carry you through the storms of opposition. You can do more than you know, and your strength will shine through.

The Connection Between Gratitude and Fortification

Gratitude plays an essential role in fortifying inner strength and can transform the way you face challenges. When you actively embrace gratitude, you shift your focus from what's lacking to what you already possess. This shift creates a powerful foundation for resilience, allowing you to confront difficulties with a renewed sense of purpose.

By recognizing and appreciating the positive aspects of your life, you cultivate a mindset that fosters courage and determination. Gratitude acts as a shield, protecting you from negativity and self-doubt that can arise during tough times. Instead of feeling overwhelmed by obstacles, you learn to view them as opportunities for growth.

Each moment of gratitude reinforces your inner armor, reminding you of your strengths and the support around you. It encourages you to acknowledge your achievements, no matter how small, and to celebrate the people and experiences that uplift you. This practice enhances your emotional well-being and strengthens your spirit, enabling you to stand firm against adversity.

When you face challenges with a grateful heart, you're less likely to succumb to despair. Instead, you become more open to solutions and possibilities. Gratitude helps you realize that light can be found even in the darkest moments.

Developing a Resilient Spirit amid Chaos

While chaos often feels overwhelming, developing a resilient spirit can empower you to navigate the storm confidently. Life's unpredictable nature can throw challenges your way. Still, fostering resilience creates an inner strength that helps you stand firm against adversity.

Start by acknowledging your feelings. It's okay to feel anxious or uncertain when chaos reigns. Embrace those emotions and understand that they're part of your human experience. Instead of resisting, allow yourself to process these feelings.

You can also practice mindfulness. Taking a few moments to breathe deeply can ground you, helping to clear your mind and focus on the present.

Another key to resilience is cultivating a supportive network. Reach out to friends or family who uplift you; share your struggles and lean on their encouragement. Sometimes, knowing you're not alone can lighten the burden and provide new perspectives.

Embrace adaptability. Life's chaos can lead to unexpected changes, and your ability to adjust your plans can greatly impact your resilience. Whether it's shifting your goals or finding new coping strategies, flexibility can transform obstacles into opportunities for growth.

Lastly, remember to celebrate small victories. Acknowledge your progress, no matter how minor it may seem. Each step strengthens your spirit, reinforcing the belief that you can endure and thrive, even in turbulent times.

The Role of Hope in Breaking Chains

Resilience provides a sturdy foundation, but hope truly lights the way forward. When caught in the chains of despair, it can feel like the world's weight is pressing down on you. Yet, hope acts as a beacon, illuminating the path to freedom. It tells you that change is possible and you're not alone in your struggles.

You might feel trapped, but hope invites you to envision a brighter future, giving you the courage to take that first step toward breaking those chains.

When you nurture hope, you cultivate the belief that your circumstances can improve. It's not about ignoring the realities of your situation; instead, it's about acknowledging them while still believing in the possibility of transformation.

Each moment you choose hope, you're choosing to empower yourself. You're saying, "I deserve more than this," that declaration alone can shift your perspective and open new doors.

Hope encourages you to seek support from friends, family, or even professional guidance. It reminds you that healing isn't meant to be a solo journey.

As you share your burdens, you'll find that hope multiplies in the presence of others, creating a community of strength.

As you embrace hope, remember that it's a powerful tool for breaking chains. It nurtures your spirit and fuels your resilience, reminding you that light can shine through even in the darkest times.

Hold onto that hope—it's your most potent armor in the battle for your spirit.

Envisioning Victory Before it Manifests

Amidst your challenges, envisioning victory before it manifests can be transformative. When you picture the desired outcome, you create a blueprint that guides your actions and fuels your spirit. This vision isn't just wishful thinking; it's a powerful tool that helps you navigate life's uncertainties with resilience and purpose.

Start by closing your eyes and imagining what success looks like for you. Visualize the emotions you'll feel, the people you'll celebrate with, and the strength you'll draw from this achievement. This vivid imagery is a motivational anchor, reminding you of your potential, especially during tough times.

When you face setbacks, revisit that vision. Let it remind you that obstacles are merely stepping stones on your path.

It's essential to couple this envisioning with actionable steps. Dreaming is crucial, but concrete actions toward your goals solidify your commitment. Break down your vision into smaller, achievable tasks, and celebrate each milestone.

This keeps you motivated and reinforces the belief that victory is within your reach.

Becoming a Conduit of Light: Radiating from Within

Becoming a conduit of light means embracing the radiance that already exists within you. This inner light is your authentic self, the essence that connects you to the universe and others around you. When you recognize and nurture this brilliance, you empower yourself and inspire those in your life.

To truly radiate from within, consider these practices:

- **Mindful Reflection**: Take time each day to reflect on your thoughts and feelings. This awareness helps you connect with your inner light.

- **Acts of Kindness**: Small, genuine gestures of compassion can amplify your light. Every act of kindness sends ripples of positivity into the world.

- **Gratitude**: Cultivating a grateful mindset shifts your focus from what's lacking to what's abundant in your life, enhancing your inner glow.

- **Surround Yourself with Positivity**: Engage with people and environments that uplift you. Positive energy is contagious and fuels your own light.

As you embrace these practices, your light will grow stronger, casting away shadows of doubt and fear.

When you shine brightly, you create a safe space for others to do the same. Remember, being a conduit of light isn't just about personal growth; it's about contributing to humanity's collective spirit.

You can illuminate the path for others, guiding them through their struggles. Embrace your role as a beacon of hope and love, and watch your world transform.

Spiritual Strength Through Physical Discipline

Many find that cultivating spiritual strength is intricately tied to physical discipline. When you engage in regular physical activity, you're not just strengthening your body but also nurturing your spirit. The connection between your physical well-being and your spiritual resilience is profound. Each time you push through a workout or commit to a healthy routine, you're building habits that foster determination, patience, and focus—essential for spiritual growth.

Engaging in physical discipline teaches you to set and achieve goals, reinforcing the mindset that you can overcome challenges. This discipline spills over into your spiritual life, helping you confront fears, doubts, and adversities more confidently. Think of every drop of sweat as a reminder that you're capable of enduring, that you can transform discomfort into strength.

Moreover, physical discipline often cultivates a sense of community. Participating in group activities or classes connects you with others with similar aspirations. This connection can support your spiritual journey, reminding you you're not alone in your struggles.

As you develop your physical strength, remember to listen to your body. Rest and recovery are just as important as the work you put in. Honoring your limits cultivates a balanced approach that nurtures your body and spirit.

Embrace this journey of physical discipline, and you'll find it becomes a powerful ally in your quest for spiritual strength.

Enduring to the End: When Victory Seems Distant

How do you keep going when victory feels like a distant dream? It's tough, isn't it? You might feel like you're fighting a never-ending battle, and the finish line seems just out of reach.

But remember, enduring through these challenging times is part of the journey. You're not alone in this struggle; many have faced similar trials and emerged stronger.

Here are some strategies to help you push through:

- **Focus on small wins**: Celebrate every little achievement; they add up and can shift your perspective.

- **Stay connected**: Lean on your support system—friends, family, or mentors. Sharing your struggles can lighten your load.

- **Practice self-compassion**: Remind yourself it's okay to feel overwhelmed. Be kind to yourself and acknowledge your efforts.

- **Visualize your goal**: Picture what victory looks like for you. Keeping that vision in mind can reignite your motivation.

When you feel like giving up, pause and breathe. Reflect on how far you've come rather than how far you still have to go.

Each challenge you face builds resilience, shaping you into someone capable of overcoming obstacles. Remember, enduring to the end doesn't mean you must do it alone.

Reach out, share your burdens, and bolster your spirit. Victory may seem distant now, but every step you take brings you closer to it. Keep the faith and trust the process.

Chapter Six

The Shadow Within: Understanding and Overcoming Inner Battles

You might find yourself in a constant struggle, caught between your primal instincts and your higher aspirations. These inner battles often manifest as self-sabotage or negative self-talk, leading to a cycle that feels impossible to break. Understanding these conflicts isn't just about acknowledging them; it's about discovering the deeper wounds that invite spiritual challenges. What if embracing humility and self-compassion is the key to overcoming these battles? As you explore this journey, you'll uncover surprising insights that can reshape your approach to your inner self and the world around you.

The Battle Against Self: Flesh vs. Spirit

When you plunge into the complexities of your inner world, you often find yourself caught in a fierce tug-of-war between the flesh and the spirit. This internal battle can feel overwhelming as your desires and instincts clash with your higher ideals and aspirations. You might crave immediate gratification—comfort from food, avoidance of responsibilities, or indulgence in distractions—yet your spirit yearns for growth, discipline, and purpose.

Understanding this conflict is vital. The flesh represents your primal instincts, often driven by short-term satisfaction and self-preservation. On the other hand, the spirit embodies your higher self, seeking enlightenment and fulfillment. Recognizing these opposing forces is the first step toward resolution. Instead of viewing them as enemies, consider them as parts of your whole, each with its own lessons to teach you.

As you navigate this internal struggle, it's important to develop self-compassion. Acknowledge that it's natural to wrestle with these conflicting desires. You're not alone in your journey; everyone grapples with similar challenges.

Cultivating mindfulness can help you become more aware of your thoughts and feelings, allowing you to discern when you're yielding to the flesh or empowering the spirit.

Ultimately, the goal isn't to eliminate one side but to find a balance. Embrace the duality within you, and work to align your actions with your spirit's calling. This harmony can lead to a more authentic and fulfilling life, enabling you to overcome the battles that arise from within.

Recognizing Patterns of Self-Sabotage

Many of us find ourselves trapped in cycles of self-sabotage, often without realizing it. You might notice these patterns manifesting in various aspects of your life—whether it's procrastinating on important projects, engaging in negative self-talk, or choosing relationships that don't serve your growth. Recognizing these behaviors is the first step toward breaking free.

Take a moment to reflect on your habits. Do you find yourself setting goals but then undermining your efforts? Maybe you start a new workout routine only to skip sessions when you feel the urge to push forward. These actions often stem from fear of failure or even fear of success, creating an internal conflict that can be difficult to navigate.

It's essential to identify the triggers that lead to self-sabotage. Are specific situations, people, or even emotions prompting you to retreat into old patterns? You can develop strategies to counteract these triggers by becoming aware of them.

For example, when you feel the urge to procrastinate, try breaking tasks into smaller, manageable steps. This approach helps reduce overwhelm and fosters a sense of accomplishment.

Inner Voices: Discerning Truth from Lies

Often, you might find yourself caught in a whirlwind of inner voices, each vying for your attention and shaping your self-perception. Some voices echo truths, but others distort reality, leaving you uncertain about your worth and direction. It's essential to discern which voices are rooted in truth and which are laced with deception.

Start by paying attention to the tone of these inner dialogues. Is a voice encouraging you to take risks and grow, or is it criticizing and belittling your efforts? Recognizing the source of these thoughts can help clarify their validity. You may notice that negative voices often stem from past experiences or external influences. At the same time, positive affirmations typically arise from your authentic self.

Next, challenge the lies. Ask yourself if these thoughts are based on facts or fears. When a voice tells you you're not enough, counter it with evidence of your achievements and strengths. Write down these truths to create a tangible reminder of your worth.

Moreover, practice mindfulness. Acknowledge the voices without judgment, then gently redirect your focus to constructive thoughts. This practice helps you distance yourself from harmful narratives, allowing you to foster a more compassionate internal dialogue.

Ultimately, discernment is about learning to trust yourself. As you navigate these inner battles, remember that you can silence the lies and amplify the truth, leading to a healthier, more fulfilling self-perception.

How Inner Wounds Attract Spiritual Attack

These wounds can distort your self-perception, leading to feelings of inadequacy or shame. You might question your worth or feel unworthy of love and support. This mindset is a beacon, attracting negative energies that thrive on your inner turmoil.

Moreover, your emotional state often affects your decisions and actions, exposing you to spiritual challenges. When you're in pain, you may seek comfort in unhealthy ways—perhaps through escapism or toxic relationships—compounding your wounds and making you an easier target for spiritual attacks.

It is vital to recognize how these inner wounds interact with your spiritual life. Addressing your pain can heal those wounds and close the openings that attract negativity.

This process involves self-reflection, seeking support, and engaging in practices that nurture your spirit, such as meditation or prayer.

The Role of Unforgiveness and Bitterness

While it might feel easier to hold onto grudges, unforgiveness and bitterness can weigh heavily on your spirit, creating barriers to healing and peace. These emotions often disguise themselves as justified responses to hurt. Still, they can actually imprison you in a cycle of pain. When you cling to past grievances, you may find that your thoughts are consumed by resentment, preventing you from moving forward.

It's important to recognize that unforgiveness affects more than emotional well-being; it can also impact physical health and relationships. Your body reacts to stress, and the burden of bitterness can lead to chronic tension, fatigue, and even illness. You may isolate yourself, pushing away those who care about you, believing that your pain is too profound for others to understand.

Instead of allowing these emotions to control your life, consider the power of forgiveness—not for the one who wronged you, but for your own freedom. Forgiveness can be a profound act of self-compassion, opening the door to healing and renewal. It doesn't mean condoning the offense; rather, it's about letting go of the weight that drags you down.

Start small. Reflect on what you've been holding onto and acknowledge the hurt. Then, gently remind yourself that you deserve peace. By choosing to release unforgiveness and bitterness, you'll begin to reclaim your spirit and foster an environment where healing can truly flourish.

Generational Curses: Breaking the Cycle

Generational curses can feel like invisible chains, binding you to patterns of behavior and trauma passed down through your family lineage. You might find yourself repeating mistakes or struggling with issues that seem to have no clear origin in your own life.

These cycles can manifest as addiction, unhealthy relationships, or even persistent feelings of inadequacy. It's crucial to recognize that while these patterns may feel overwhelming, they don't have to define your future.

Breaking the cycle starts with awareness. Acknowledge the behaviors or beliefs that you've inherited, and consider how they impact your life today. This isn't about placing blame but understanding your struggles' roots.

Reflect on your family history, and identify specific instances that resonate with your experiences.

Next, seek healing through open communication. Talk to family members about your shared history and express how these patterns affect you. This dialogue can foster understanding and create a supportive environment for change.

Then, embrace personal growth. Engage in practices that promote self-awareness, such as journaling, therapy, or spiritual guidance.

These tools can help you develop new perspectives, allowing you to break free from limiting beliefs.

Freedom from Guilt, Shame, and Regret

Carrying the weight of guilt, shame, and regret can feel like a heavy burden dragging you down, obscuring the path to your true self. These feelings often stem from past mistakes or perceived failures, creating a cycle of self-judgment that's hard to escape.

Recognizing these emotions are common human experiences is the first step toward liberation. You're not alone in this struggle.

To begin your journey toward freedom, it's crucial to confront these feelings head-on. Reflect on the sources of your guilt and shame. Are they rooted in your own values or imposed by others? Understanding this distinction can help you reclaim your narrative.

Acknowledge your feelings without letting them define you. They're experiences, not your identity.

Next, practice self-compassion. Treat yourself with the kindness you'd offer a friend in a similar situation. Remind yourself that everyone makes mistakes, but they don't diminish your worth.

Allow yourself to learn from these experiences rather than be imprisoned by them.

Finally, consider forgiveness—both of yourself and others. This doesn't mean condoning past actions but releasing their hold on your spirit.

Engage in positive affirmations and surround yourself with supportive individuals who encourage growth.

Letting Go of Fear: The Root of Many Battles

Fear often acts as an invisible barrier, keeping you from reaching your full potential and pursuing your dreams. It creeps in, whispering doubts and uncertainties that can paralyze your spirit. You might hesitate to take risks, avoid new opportunities, or even shy away from expressing your true self. This fear isn't just a minor inconvenience; it can shape your decisions and hinder your growth.

Analyzing the root of your fears can be a transformative experience. What are you truly afraid of? Is it judgment, failure, or perhaps the unknown? Understanding the source of your fear helps you realize that it often stems from past experiences or ingrained beliefs rather than a reflection of your current reality. When you confront these fears head-on, you strip away their power.

Support is essential during this process. Surround yourself with positive influences—people who encourage and empower you. Engage in practices that cultivate courage, whether through journaling, meditation, or seeking guidance through spiritual means. Acknowledge your fear, but don't let it define you. Instead, allow it to become a catalyst for growth.

Letting go of fear isn't about eliminating it entirely; it's about learning to manage it. As you take small steps toward facing your fears, you'll discover resilience and strength within you. Embrace the journey, knowing that every effort you make to overcome fear brings you closer to your authentic self and the life you were meant to live.

Replacing Negative Self-Talk with Divine Truth

Many people struggle with negative self-talk, a relentless inner critic that undermines their confidence and self-worth. This inner dialogue often tells them they're not good enough, smart enough, or worthy of love. It's a harsh narrative that can lead to feelings of inadequacy and despair.

But you can challenge this negativity by replacing those damaging thoughts with divine truth. Start by recognizing when those negative thoughts arise. Acknowledge them without judgment. Once you identify these patterns, counter them with affirmations rooted in truth. For instance, when you hear, "I'm a failure," replace it with, "I am growing and learning." Instead of "I don't deserve happiness," affirm, "I am worthy of joy and love." These truths, often found in spiritual teachings, can help reshape your self-perception.

It's essential to be patient with yourself during this process. Changing deeply ingrained thought patterns takes time and practice. Surround yourself with supportive influences—books, podcasts, or communities reinforcing positive beliefs.

You might also consider journaling, where you can document your struggles and victories. This practice helps clarify your thoughts and allows you to see your growth over time.

The Healing Power of Acceptance and Grace

Acceptance and grace can transform your inner landscape, healing where pain once resided. When you embrace these two powerful forces, you create space for growth and resilience. Instead of resisting your feelings, you allow yourself to acknowledge them, leading to a deeper understanding of your inner battles.

Here are four ways acceptance and grace can help you heal:

1. **Embracing Reality**: Accepting your circumstances as they are, not as you wish, helps you confront challenges head-on. This clarity fosters empowerment, allowing you to take actionable steps toward change.

2. **Letting Go of Judgment**: Grace teaches you to release self-criticism. When you stop judging yourself harshly, you create a nurturing environment where healing can thrive. You deserve compassion, especially from yourself.

3. **Cultivating Patience**: Acceptance encourages patience with your healing journey. Change takes time, and recognizing that fosters a more forgiving mindset. You're not in a race; you're on a personal journey.

4. **Building Connection**: Sharing your experiences with others fosters a sense of community. Acceptance opens the door to vulnerability, allowing you to connect deeper. This connection can

provide invaluable support during tough times.

Unmasking the Spirit of Rebellion

While feeling a sense of rebellion against expectations or limitations is natural, understanding this spirit within you can be a path to self-discovery and empowerment.

You may question authority, norms, or even your beliefs, and that's okay. This inner rebellion often stems from a desire for authenticity and freedom. It's an instinctive reaction to feeling confined but can also be a powerful catalyst for change.

As you explore this spirit of rebellion, ask yourself what motivates it. Are you rebelling against someone else's expectations or seeking your own identity? Recognizing the root of your rebellion can help you harness its energy constructively.

Instead of acting impulsively, channel that energy into creative outlets or personal growth. This way, you gain clarity on your values and desires.

It's essential to distinguish between healthy rebellion and destructive opposition. While it's empowering to stand up for yourself, consider how your actions affect your relationships and goals.

Embrace an attitude of reflection rather than reaction. When you feel that urge to push back, take a moment to breathe and evaluate the situation.

Dealing with Pride: The Hidden Enemy Within

Rebellion can often lead to a confrontation with another powerful force: pride. This hidden enemy can subtly infiltrate your thoughts and feelings, influencing your decisions and interactions.

It's easy to underestimate its impact, but pride can distort your perception of self and others, creating barriers that hinder growth and connection. Recognizing pride in your life is the first step toward overcoming it.

Here are four signs to watch for:

1. **Defensiveness**: Are you quick to justify your actions or dismiss criticism? This reaction often stems from pride and prevents you from seeing valuable perspectives.

2. **Comparisons**: Do you frequently measure your worth against others? This mindset can keep you trapped in a cycle of jealousy and discontent.

3. **Difficulty Apologizing**: Is saying "I'm sorry" challenging for you? Pride can make humility feel like a loss, but it's vital to healthy relationships.

4. **Fear of Vulnerability**: Do you struggle to show your true self? Pride often convinces you that revealing your weaknesses is a sign of failure when, in reality, it's a pathway to authentic connections.

As you confront these indicators, remember that acknowledging pride isn't a sign of weakness; it's a courageous step toward self-awareness and spiritual growth.

Embrace this journey with compassion for yourself, knowing that each challenge you face is an opportunity for transformation.

Cultivating a Humble and Teachable Heart

Embracing humility can profoundly transform your life. When you cultivate a humble and teachable heart, you open yourself to growth and deeper connections with others.

Humility allows you to recognize your limitations and understand that you don't have all the answers. This perspective creates a fertile ground for learning, helping you to receive wisdom from various sources, including those you mightn't expect.

You might sometimes resist humility, seeing it as a weakness. However, it's important to shift that mindset. A humble heart is strong; it enables you to confront your inner battles without the armor of pride.

By letting down your defenses, you invite honest feedback and constructive criticism, vital tools for personal development.

To cultivate this heart, start by practicing active listening. When others speak, truly hear them without formulating your response right away.

Acknowledge their perspectives, which can reveal insights you might've overlooked. Additionally, embrace vulnerability. Share your struggles and ask for help when you need it.

This strengthens your relationships and fosters a supportive environment where growth can thrive.

The Role of Repentance and Renewal

Repentance and renewal are essential processes that allow you to break free from the cycles of regret and stagnation. When you acknowledge your missteps and seek to turn away from them, you open the door to personal transformation.

This journey isn't always easy, but it can lead to a more fulfilling life.

Here are four key aspects to contemplate as you embrace repentance and renewal:

1. **Self-Reflection**: Take time to examine your thoughts, actions, and their impact on yourself and others. Understanding where you've strayed can provide clarity and a path forward.

2. **Sincere Apology**: If your actions have hurt others, a heartfelt apology can be a powerful step towards healing. This isn't just about apologizing; it's about demonstrating genuine remorse and a commitment to change.

3. **Commitment to Change**: Repentance isn't just an acknowledgment of wrongdoing; it's a promise to do better. Identify specific changes you can make to avoid repeating past mistakes.

4. **Seek Support**: Surround yourself with a supportive community. Whether it's friends, family, or a spiritual leader, having people who can guide and encourage you will strengthen your resolve.

Walking in the Spirit: A Lifestyle of Overcoming

Walking in the Spirit isn't just a lofty ideal; it's a practical way to navigate life's challenges and overcome obstacles. It invites a deeper connection with your inner strength and divine guidance. This lifestyle means leaning on the Spirit's wisdom to make decisions, respond to trials, and find peace amid chaos.

Recognizing the presence of the Spirit in your daily life can transform how you approach struggles. Instead of feeling overwhelmed, you can find hope and resilience. You can rely on that inner voice when temptations arise, guiding you away from destructive patterns. It's not about perfection but progress—about making conscious choices that align with your spiritual values.

You might encounter setbacks, but don't let them discourage you. Each moment presents a new opportunity to realign and recommit to walking in the Spirit. Practicing mindfulness and prayer can help deepen this connection. Remember, you're not alone in this journey; the Spirit is there to assist, comfort, and empower you.

As you cultivate this lifestyle, you'll notice a shift in your perspective. Challenges become less intimidating, and you'll be equipped to tackle them gracefully. Trust that walking in the Spirit nurtures your spirit, fostering a sense of peace that transcends external circumstances.

Embrace this journey, and watch how it transforms your inner battles into victories of the soul.

Chapter Seven

Waging War in Prayer: Strategies for Spiritual Breakthrough

You might often find yourself overwhelmed by the challenges of spiritual warfare, wondering how to effectively engage in prayer that truly makes an impact. Understanding what makes prayer powerful can transform your approach, allowing you to harness the strength of declaration and supplication. By incorporating scripture and intercessory prayer, you're fortifying your spirit and creating a ripple effect in your community. As you navigate the complexities of maintaining a consistent prayer life, you may uncover strategies that lead to profound breakthroughs. What if you could reveal the secrets to sustaining your spiritual strength in the face of intense battles?

What Makes a Prayer Powerful?

When you think about what makes a prayer powerful, consider the heart behind it. It's not just the words you say; it's the authenticity and fervor that fuel those words. A prayer becomes potent when it flows from a place of genuine faith and vulnerability. When you pour out your soul, you invite divine intervention, opening the door to transformation.

Your intentions matter immensely. If your heart beats for change, your prayers will resonate with passion. They'll carry the weight of your desires, fears, and hopes, creating an undeniable connection with the Divine. This connection isn't about formality; it's about raw honesty. Speak from your heart, share your struggles, and let your spirit cry out.

Don't underestimate the power of gratitude in your prayers. When you express thankfulness, you shift your focus from your burdens to the blessings surrounding you. This shift amplifies your faith and aligns you with divine possibilities.

Moreover, persistence is essential. A powerful prayer isn't always answered instantly, and that's okay. Keep knocking, keep seeking, and keep believing. Each moment spent in prayer is an investment in your spiritual journey, forging resilience and deepening your relationship with God.

Prayers of Declaration vs. Supplication

Prayers of declaration and supplication serve distinct yet powerful purposes in your spiritual journey. When you declare, you're not just speaking words but asserting the truth of God's promises and your identity in Christ. This bold proclamation of faith claims the victories already won in the spiritual domain.

You align your mindset with God's perspective through declarations, empowering you to rise above doubt and fear. It's like wielding a sword, cutting through the lies that seek to bind you.

On the other hand, supplication is an earnest petition, a heartfelt cry for God's intervention. It's where vulnerability meets trust, as you bring your needs and desires before God. In these moments, you acknowledge your dependence on Him, seek His guidance, and invite His presence into your circumstances.

Supplication fosters intimacy in your relationship with God, reminding you that you're not alone in your struggles.

Both forms of prayer are essential; they complement each other beautifully. While declarations build your faith, supplications open the door for divine assistance. You can declare God's promises over your life and simultaneously humbly bring your requests before Him.

This dynamic interplay enhances your spiritual warfare, arming you with confidence and reliance. Embrace the power of declaration and supplication, knowing each is crucial in your journey toward a spiritual breakthrough.

With these tools in hand, you're equipped to face any challenge that comes your way.

Using Scripture in Prayer: Precision and Power

Scripture's power becomes an essential ally in your prayer life, transforming your conversations with God into dynamic encounters. When you weave God's Word into your prayers, you're not just reciting verses but declaring truths that resonate in the spiritual domain. This precision in using Scripture can sharpen your focus and amplify your faith, preparing you for the battles ahead.

Think of your prayers as arrows and Scripture as the bow. Each verse you invoke empowers you to strike with purpose, targeting the specific strongholds in your life and the lives of others. For instance, when you face anxiety, claiming Philippians 4:6-7 reminds you to be anxious for nothing, allowing God's peace to guard your heart. You affirm your trust in His promises each time you speak these words.

Moreover, using Scripture in prayer equips you to combat the enemy's lies. When doubt creeps in, declaring Romans 8:31—"If God is for us, who can be against us?"—fortifies your spirit and reminds you of the unwavering support of your Creator.

As you immerse yourself in God's Word, you'll find that it becomes a wellspring of strength and clarity. Let Scripture guide your prayers, and watch as your spiritual life ignites with renewed vigor.

You're not just praying but engaging in a powerful dialogue that shifts the atmosphere, bringing heaven's reality into your present circumstances. Embrace this practice, and let the precision of Scripture fuel your spiritual breakthroughs.

The Role of Intercessory Prayer

Intercessory prayer is a powerful pillar in the spiritual journey, offering an essential connection not just between you and God but also among believers. When you engage in intercessory prayer, you step into a profound role—one that transcends your personal needs and reaches out to others. This act of praying on behalf of others fosters unity and strengthens the spiritual fabric of your community.

Here are four key roles of intercessory prayer:

1. **Advocacy**: You become an advocate for those who may be struggling or unable to pray for themselves, standing in the gap and lifting their burdens before God.

2. **Strengthening Faith**: As you intercede, you empower others and bolster your own faith. Witnessing God's responses to your

prayers can deepen your trust in His promises.

3. **Spiritual Warfare**: Intercessory prayer serves as a weapon against spiritual attacks. You're actively battling for hearts and minds, declaring victory over darkness.

4. **Community Building**: It creates a sense of belonging and support within your faith community, encouraging others to pray and share their struggles fostering deeper connections.

As you embrace the role of an intercessor, remember that your prayers can shift the atmosphere, heal wounds, and bring hope.

Let your heart be stirred with compassion, knowing that through intercessory prayer, you can be a catalyst for change in the lives of others and in the world around you.

Prayers for Protection and Strength

Protection and strength are essential to our spiritual journey, providing a foundation to confidently stand against life's challenges. When you seek divine shelter and fortitude, you're not just asking for help but declaring your intent to face the world with unwavering faith.

Prayers for protection and strength can be powerful weapons in your spiritual arsenal, allowing you to confront fears and uncertainties with courage. Start by inviting God into your heart. Speak openly about your vulnerabilities and needs. You might pray, "Lord, surround me with Your protection. Shield me from negativity and doubt."

This simple yet profound request affirms your reliance on divine support and strengthens your resolve. As you articulate your desires, visualize a protective barrier enveloping you, empowering you to embrace your challenges head-on.

Remember to ask for strength as well. "Grant me the strength to overcome obstacles and to stand firm in my faith" can be an empowering declaration. Recognizing your limitations while seeking divine assistance helps you cultivate resilience.

As you pray, remember that strength isn't just physical; it's mental, emotional, and spiritual. Incorporate these prayers into your daily routine. Consistency deepens your connection with the Divine and fortifies your spirit.

Trust that your prayers are heard, and let them remind you that protection and strength are always within your reach, waiting to uplift you in your spiritual battles.

Overcoming Obstacles to Effective Prayer

Even as you seek protection and strength through prayer, you may encounter obstacles that hinder your communication with the Divine. Recognizing these barriers is the first step in overcoming them and reclaiming your spiritual power.

Here are four common obstacles you might face:

1. **Distraction**: Life's chaos can distract you from prayer. Carve out a quiet space and time to connect deeply with your spirit.

2. **Doubt**: Questioning your worthiness or the effectiveness of your prayers can cloud your faith. Remind yourself that you're deserving of divine connection and intervention.

3. **Unforgiveness**: Holding onto grudges can create emotional blockages, preventing your prayers from reaching their intended

destination. Seek to let go, allowing love and compassion to flow through you.

4. **Fear**: Fear of the unknown or fear of vulnerability can stifle your prayers. Embrace the courage to lay your fears before the Divine, trusting in a power greater than yourself.

Understanding and Breaking Prayer Blockages

Prayer blockages can feel like heavy weights pulling you down, stifling your spiritual growth. You may find yourself wrestling with distractions, doubts, or even feelings of unworthiness. These blockages can create a barrier between you and the divine, making it seem impossible to connect in prayer. But understanding these obstacles is the first step to breaking free.

Start by identifying the root causes. Are there unresolved issues in your life? Unforgiveness? Negative thought patterns? Acknowledging these barriers can empower you to confront them head-on. Remember, you're not alone in this battle—many have faced similar struggles, and victory is possible.

Next, examine your prayer life. Are you approaching prayer with a sense of obligation rather than a desire for connection? Shift your mindset. Treat prayer as a conversation with a loving friend, not a chore. This change in perspective can ignite passion and open your heart to deeper communication.

Incorporate fasting, worship, and scripture into your prayer routine. These practices can break the chains of blockages and create a more open channel for divine guidance.

Seek support from your community; sharing your struggles can lead to breakthroughs you couldn't achieve alone.

Praying for Deliverance and Healing

Deliverance and healing are powerful aspects of spiritual warfare that can transform your life. When you pray for deliverance, you're not just seeking to rid yourself of negative influences but inviting God's light into every dark corner of your spirit.

Healing prayer goes beyond physical ailments, addressing emotional and spiritual wounds that hinder your purpose. Here's how you can engage in this transformative prayer:

1. **Identify Strongholds**: Reflect on areas where you feel trapped or burdened. Acknowledge these strongholds, whether they be fear, addiction, or unforgiveness.

2. **Seek God's Presence**: Create a sacred space for prayer. Invite God into your situation with a heart open to His guidance and love. You'll find that His presence can provide clarity and strength.

3. **Declare His Word**: Use scripture to declare God's promises over your life. Verses about healing and deliverance can serve as powerful affirmations that reinforce your faith.

4. **Pray with Authority**: Remember to command freedom and healing in Jesus' name. Speak boldly, and refuse to accept anything less than God's best for your life.

As you immerse yourself in this process, know that deliverance and healing aren't just one-time events but ongoing journeys.

Trust in the transformative power of prayer, and watch as your spirit flourishes and your life takes on a new, vibrant purpose.

Standing in the Gap: Praying for the Vulnerable

In a world filled with challenges and injustices, the call to stand in the gap for the vulnerable resonates deeply within our spirits. You have the power to intercede for those who can't fight for themselves—children in poverty, the oppressed, the marginalized. Your prayers can become a lifeline, a beacon of hope that pierces through darkness and despair.

When you pray for the vulnerable, you're not just asking for change but engaging in a spiritual battle. You're wielding the authority granted to you as a believer, calling forth protection, provision, and liberation. It's about feeling the weight of their struggles on your heart and refusing to turn a blind eye. You're standing in the gap, bridging the divide between despair and hope.

As you pray, visualize those you're lifting up. Picture their faces, hear their cries, and let their pain ignite a fire within you. Every prayer you utter sends ripples through the spiritual dimension, dismantling strongholds and inviting divine intervention.

You're not alone in this; the Holy Spirit empowers your prayers, aligning them with God's heart for justice and mercy.

Warring Tongues: The Language of Spiritual Combat

Release the power of your words, for they serve as weapons in spiritual combat. Every declaration you make, every prayer you utter, carries the potential to shift the atmosphere around you. When you engage in spiritual warfare, your tongue becomes a sword, cutting through the darkness and establishing God's kingdom on earth.

Here's how you can harness this divine language effectively:

1. **Speak Scripture**: The Word of God is your ultimate weapon. Declare His promises over your life and the lives of others. When you speak His truth, you create an unshakeable foundation.

2. **Pray in the Spirit**: Allow the Holy Spirit to guide your prayers. When you pray in tongues, you tap into a heavenly language that empowers your spirit and confuses the enemy.

3. **Declare Victory**: Don't just ask for help; proclaim victory over your battles. Your declarations of faith and triumph can break strongholds and establish God's will.

4. **Use Specific Intent**: Be intentional with your words. Identify the battles you face and articulate your prayers with clarity. Focus on specific areas where you seek breakthroughs, whether healing, provision, or deliverance.

Your tongue is a powerful tool in the fight against darkness. By employing these strategies, you can wade deeper into spiritual warfare, claim victories, and advance the kingdom.

The Role of Fasting in Intensifying Prayer

Fasting is like a spiritual amplifier, intensifying your prayers and sharpening your focus on God. When you set aside food and other distractions, you create space for deeper communion with Him. In this sacred stillness, you can hear His voice more clearly and align your heart with His will.

Fasting heightens your awareness of spiritual realities, empowering you to confront the battles within and around you. As you fast, you're not merely abstaining from physical nourishment but inviting God's presence into your struggle. You're declaring that your need for Him surpasses any earthly craving.

This surrender reminds you that your strength comes not from what you consume but from the very breath of God. When you couple fasting with prayer, you release a dynamic force that transforms circumstances and shifts spiritual atmospheres.

Moreover, fasting cultivates humility and dependence on God. It strips away the clutter of everyday life, allowing you to confront the spiritual strongholds that may be holding you back. You're more open to receiving His guidance and wisdom in this vulnerable state.

Prayers for Families and Households

When you gather your family in prayer, you create a powerful fortress against the spiritual battles that threaten your household. This collective act strengthens your bond and invites divine protection and guidance into your lives.

Engaging in family prayer equips you to confront the challenges and temptations that may arise, ensuring that your home remains a sanctuary of peace and love.

To effectively wage spiritual warfare for your family, consider incorporating these four focused prayer strategies:

1. **Pray for Unity**: Ask God to bind your hearts together in love and understanding, dispelling any discord that may arise. A united family stands strong against spiritual attacks.

2. **Cover Each Member**: Pray for each family member, asking for divine protection, wisdom, and strength. Personal prayers create a sense of belonging and individual support.

3. **Break Generational Curses**: Identify and renounce any negative patterns or spiritual strongholds that may have affected your lineage. Declare freedom and healing over your family line.

4. **Invite the Holy Spirit**: Seek the guidance and presence of the Holy Spirit in your home. His wisdom can illuminate paths and decisions, helping you navigate life's complexities.

Spiritual Warfare in Corporate Prayer

Gathering in corporate prayer magnifies the spiritual power of collective faith and intent. When you join others in prayer, you create a dynamic atmosphere where faith amplifies and strongholds are shaken. Each voice adds a layer of intensity, creating a force that can penetrate the spiritual domain. You're not just praying as an individual; you're part of a unified front, standing together against the adversary.

In this collective effort, you harness the strength of community, drawing on the shared experiences and burdens of those around you. Remember, where two or three are gathered, He's in the midst (Matthew 18:20). You invoke His presence and authority, aligning your hearts and minds in fervent petition.

As you pray together, you can cover a wider range of issues, addressing issues that affect your community, families, and even nations.

Moreover, corporate prayer can lead to deeper revelations and insights as you listen to the Spirit's guidance through one another. Each person may receive distinct visions or words that, when woven together, create a clearer picture of God's will.

This is where spiritual warfare becomes a battle and a strategic campaign.

How to Pray Through Spiritual Silence

In the quiet moments of spiritual silence, you might feel an unsettling stillness, as if the heavens are closed off. This can be disheartening, but it's crucial to remember that spiritual silence isn't a void; it's an opportunity for deeper engagement.

You can transform this silence into a powerful prayer experience by employing these strategies:

1. **Embrace Stillness**: Allow yourself to sit in the discomfort. Acknowledge the silence without rushing to fill it with words. This is where God often speaks the loudest.

2. **Meditate on Scripture**: Choose a passage that resonates with you. Let its truth wash over you, and use it as a foundation for your prayer. This can open your heart to God's voice.

3. **Practice Gratitude**: Shift your focus from what feels absent to what you're thankful for. Make a list of blessings, no matter how small. Gratitude can break through the silence and invite peace.

4. **Listen Actively**: Instead of talking, dedicate a portion of your prayer time to listening. Be still and open your heart to receive any impressions or thoughts that come to mind.

When you commit to these practices, you'll find that spiritual silence can lead to profound breakthroughs.

In these moments of stillness, you can deepen your relationship with God, cultivate resilience, and prepare for the battles ahead.

Embrace the silence, for it's often a precursor to powerful spiritual revelations.

Sustaining a Prayer Life During Intense Warfare

Spiritual silence can feel intimidating, especially when you're facing intense spiritual warfare. You might feel overwhelmed and question whether your prayers even matter. But remember, it's in these moments that your connection to God can deepen.

First and foremost, commit to consistency to sustain your prayer life during these turbulent times. Set aside specific times each day to pray, even if it's just for a few minutes. This establishes a rhythm that helps you anchor your spirit amidst chaos.

Next, don't underestimate the power of Scripture. Meditate on verses that speak to your situation. Write them down, recite them, and let them strengthen your heart. They act as spiritual armor, fortifying your resolve.

Consider incorporating worship music into your routine. Let the melodies and lyrics lift your spirit and redirect your focus toward God's promises.

When words fail you, embrace silence. Don't shy away from stillness; use it to listen for God's guidance. He often speaks in the quiet moments.

In times of distress, reach out to your community. Share your struggles with fellow believers who can pray alongside you, reinforcing your commitment to a shared spiritual journey.

Lastly, never forget the importance of gratitude. Thank God for His presence, even in the storm. This simple act shifts your perspective and reminds you that He's always in control.

Chapter Eight

Weapons of Light: Overcoming Darkness with Divine Authority

Understanding your identity in Christ is a critical foundation for overcoming darkness in your journey through spiritual warfare. You'll discover how speaking life into situations can transform your perspective and the environment around you. As you reflect on the authority you've been given, consider how love can dissolve spiritual oppression. What does it mean to truly walk in this authority, and how can you harness it effectively? The answers may challenge your current perceptions and open doors to a deeper understanding of your role in these battles.

Understanding Your Identity in the Battle

Amid spiritual warfare, it is vital to wake up to the truth of who you are in Christ. You're not just a bystander in this battle but a warrior equipped with divine authority. Ephesians 2:10 reminds you that you're God's handiwork, created for good works. Your identity isn't defined by your past mistakes or current struggles; it's rooted in your relationship with Him. You're chosen, beloved, and empowered to stand firm against the enemy's schemes.

Understanding your identity is paramount for victory. When you know you're a child of the Most High, fear and doubt lose their grip. Romans 8:37 declares that you're more than a conqueror through Him who loves you. This isn't just a comforting thought; it's a powerful truth that can transform your perspective.

Each day, remind yourself that you wear the armor of God (Ephesians 6:10-18) and wield the sword of the Spirit.

In the heat of the battle, declare your identity aloud. Speak God's promises over yourself and believe in the authority He's given you. You're not fighting for victory; you're fighting for victory. As you embrace who you truly are, you'll find strength in your spirit and clarity in your path.

Stand tall and unshakeable, knowing that your identity in Christ is your greatest weapon against the darkness. You've been called to rise and shine, reflecting His glory as you navigate the challenges ahead.

The Power of Speaking Life Over Situations

Speak life into your circumstances, and watch the transformation unfold. As scripture reminds us, your words hold incredible power: "Death and life are in the power of the tongue" (Proverbs 18:21). When you choose to speak life, you align yourself with God's promises and create pathways for His blessings to flow.

Consider these five powerful affirmations you can declare over your situations:

- I am more than a conqueror (Romans 8:37).

- God's plans for me are good (Jeremiah 29:11).

- I have the mind of Christ (1 Corinthians 2:16).

- I am healed by His stripes (Isaiah 53:5).

- I walk in victory, not defeat (1 John 5:4).

By declaring these truths, you shift your perspective from despair to hope. Each affirmation serves as a shield against negativity and doubt, empowering you to rise above your challenges.

Remember, God created the world through His spoken word, and you can do the same.

As you practice speaking life, you'll uplift your own spirit and influence those around you. Your words can ignite faith, encourage others, and bring light into the darkest situations.

Walking in Authority: What It Really Means

When you embrace your God-given authority, you release the power to change your circumstances and influence the world around you. Walking in authority means recognizing that you're not just a passive observer in life's battles but an active participant equipped with divine power.

Scripture reminds us in Luke 10:19 that you have been given authority to trample on serpents and scorpions, symbolizing your dominion over darkness.

This authority isn't about exerting control over others; it's about aligning yourself with God's will and His purpose for your life. It's a call to rise up, speak the truth, and act with boldness. When you declare God's promises, you're not merely echoing words; you're engaging in spiritual warfare. Your voice carries weight, and your actions can shift the atmosphere around you.

Walking in authority also means understanding your identity as a child of the King. You're not defined by your past mistakes or the opinions of others. Instead, you're empowered by the knowledge that you're fearfully and wonderfully made (Psalm 139:14).

This identity fuels your confidence as you step into every situation, knowing that you carry the light of Christ within you.

How Love Dissolves Spiritual Oppression

Love's transformative power serves as a powerful weapon against spiritual oppression. When you embrace love, you create a force field that darkness can't penetrate. The love you cultivate within yourself and extend to others acts as a divine shield, breaking chains of fear, despair, and oppression. This isn't just a sentiment—it's an active choice that brings freedom and healing.

Here's how love can dissolve spiritual oppression in your life:

- **Fosters Forgiveness**: Love allows you to release grudges, freeing your heart from bitterness.

- **Encourages Connection**: It helps you build relationships that uplift and support one another.

- **Empowers Compassion**: Love inspires you to reach out to those in need, breaking down walls of isolation.

- **Ignites Hope**: In the presence of love, despair loses its grip, and you can see brighter possibilities.

- **Radiates Light**: Your love becomes a beacon that dispels darkness, inviting others to experience the same.

As you embody love, you reflect the heart of God, whose love itself (1 John 4:8). Embracing this divine love equips you to stand firm against oppression, allowing you to walk in the authority granted to you.

The Word of God: Sword of the Spirit

The Word of God is the ultimate weapon in your spiritual arsenal, cutting through the darkness with precision and power. Hebrews 4:12 reminds you that "the word of God is alive and active. Sharper than any double-edged sword." When you wield scripture, you're not just reciting words but releasing divine authority in your battles. Each verse carries the weight of truth, piercing through lies and illusions that the enemy tries to impose upon you.

In moments of doubt or despair, remember the promise of Isaiah 55:11, which assures you that God's Word won't return void. It goes forth purposefully, bringing forth life, healing, and restoration. You can stand firm, knowing that as you declare His Word, you establish a spiritual stronghold against the forces of darkness.

When faced with temptation, recall Jesus's example in the wilderness, when He wielded scripture as His shield. He showed you that the Word is your defense against the enemy's schemes. Ephesians 6:17 calls it "the sword of the Spirit," emphasizing its vital role in your armor.

Every time you meditate on or speak the Word, you engage in powerful, transformative warfare. You invite God's presence and authority into your life, driving back the shadows that seek to overwhelm you.

Aligning Actions with Words for Victory

Wielding the Word of God is powerful, but true victory comes when your actions align with those declarations. It's not enough to speak scripture; you must live it out with conviction. Your faith is a living testimony; aligning your actions with your words can break strongholds and transform lives.

Remember, "Faith without works is dead" (James 2:26).

Here are some key steps to guarantee your actions reflect your beliefs:

- **Pray with Purpose**: Seek God's guidance in everything you do. Prayer aligns your heart with His will.

- **Live Authentically**: Your lifestyle should mirror the principles you preach. Let your light shine (Matthew 5:16).

- **Serve Others**: Acts of kindness and service demonstrate the love of Christ in action.

- **Stay Accountable**: Surround yourself with believers who encourage you to walk the talk. Iron sharpens iron (Proverbs 27:17).

- **Embrace Perseverance**: Victory often requires endurance. Keep pressing on, knowing that God is with you (Philippians 3:14).

You'll find a newfound strength when your words and actions are in harmony. You'll become a powerful vessel for God's work; darkness can't stand against you.

Breaking Chains Through Acts of Kindness

Acts of kindness can serve as powerful tools for breaking the chains that bind both you and others. When you reach out in love and compassion, you manifest the grace God has bestowed upon you. Each small act, whether a smile, a helping hand, or a word of encouragement, can release a wave of liberation.

Remember the scripture that says, "For the law of the Spirit of life has set you free" (Romans 8:2). By embodying this freedom, you uplift yourself and illuminate the path for those around you.

Your kindness can dismantle walls of despair and loneliness. When you choose to bless others, you reflect the heart of Christ, who came to serve. Acts of kindness are a powerful demonstration of your faith, allowing you to break through spiritual barriers that may have held you captive.

Each time you extend grace to someone in need, you contribute to a divine chain reaction of love and healing. As you engage in these acts, don't underestimate their impact. Even the smallest gesture can ignite hope in a weary heart.

You're not just changing lives; you're engaging in spiritual warfare, wielding kindness as a weapon against the darkness. Let your hands be instruments of His peace. Stand firm in your purpose, knowing that through your kindness, chains are broken, and hearts are mended.

In this way, you become a beacon of light, illuminating how others can find their own freedom in Christ.

Countering Darkness with the Light of Truth

Often, we face the shadows of doubt and despair, but we must remember that truth is a powerful weapon against darkness. When you stand firm in the light of truth, you illuminate the lies that seek to ensnare you.

God's Word is your sword, cutting through every whisper of negativity. Embrace the truth and let it guide you in the battles of the spirit.

Here are some ways to counter darkness with the light of truth:

- **Know Your Identity**: Remember, you're fearfully and wonderfully made (Psalm 139:14). Embrace your worth.

- **Speak the Word**: Proclaim God's promises. His words carry authority and can dismantle strongholds (2 Corinthians 10:4).

- **Surround Yourself with Truth**: Engage with scripture, uplifting music, and encouraging community. They fortify your spirit.

- **Pray with Boldness**: Approach God confidently, expressing your fears and doubts. His truth will replace them with hope (Philippians 4:6-7).

- **Act on Truth**: Live out the truth you know. Your actions can be a beacon of light to others in darkness (Matthew 5:16).

When you actively counter darkness with the light of truth, you're not just fighting for yourself but creating hope for those around you.

Practicing Righteousness: Making the Enemy Flee

Practicing righteousness is a powerful way to make the enemy flee, and it starts with a single decision each day. When you walk in alignment with God's will, you activate a divine force that disrupts the plans of darkness.

Scripture reminds us in James 4:7, "Submit yourselves consequently to God. Resist the devil, and he'll flee from you." Your commitment to righteousness becomes a shield, and the enemy is disarmed in its presence.

Every moment offers you a chance to reflect the light of Christ. As you engage in acts of kindness, demonstrate love, and pursue justice, you're not just living righteously but declaring war on the forces that seek to oppress.

Ephesians 5:8 says, "For you were once darkness, but now you're light in the Lord. Walk as children of light." Embrace this identity! Each righteous choice you make pushes back the shadows.

How Integrity Dismantles Deception

Integrity serves as your spiritual armor, effectively dismantling the enemy's web of deception. When you stand firm in your integrity, you shine a light that exposes lies and reveals the truth. The enemy thrives in darkness, but your commitment to honesty and righteousness sends a powerful message that deception has no place in your life.

Embracing integrity equips you to tackle the challenges of spiritual warfare. Here are some ways it empowers you:

- **Clarity of Purpose**: You know who you are in Christ and what you stand for.

- **Strengthened Relationships**: Honesty fosters trust, allowing you to build supportive connections in your spiritual journey.

- **Enhanced Discernment**: With a clear conscience, you can better recognize the enemy's tactics.

- **Fearlessness in Confrontation**: Integrity gives you the courage to face challenges head-on, knowing you're grounded in truth.

- **Peace of Mind**: Living in alignment with your values brings peace, making it harder for the enemy to disturb your spirit.

As you cultivate integrity, remember that God's Word is your foundation. Proverbs 10:9 reminds you, "Whoever walks in integrity walks securely."

Let this inspire you to embrace integrity as a guiding principle. Stand firm, illuminated by the light of truth, and watch as deception crumbles before your unwavering spirit. Your integrity protects you and empowers you to be a beacon of hope and truth in a world desperate for light.

Standing Against Injustice with Courage

When faced with injustice, you may feel overwhelmed, but take heart! No matter how small, every act of courage contributes to the fight against darkness.

Stand firm in your beliefs and advocate for those who can't speak for themselves. Your voice has power, and your actions can inspire others to join you in this noble quest.

Look to the example of David, who faced Goliath not with fear, but with faith and determination.

He understood that true courage comes from trusting in God's strength. You, too, can draw from that same well of divine authority.

Walking in Divine Purpose and Clarity

Embracing your divine purpose brings clarity and direction to your life. When you align yourself with God's intentions for you, you harness the power that transcends earthly struggles. This divine alignment helps you navigate the complexities of life with confidence and assurance, knowing you're part of a greater plan.

To walk in your divine purpose, consider these empowering steps:

- **Seek His Guidance**: Regularly pray and meditate on Scripture. James 1:5 reminds us, "If any of you lacks wisdom, let him ask of God..."

- **Know Your Gifts**: Identify the unique talents God has given you. Romans 12:6 encourages us to use our gifts according to the grace given to us.

- **Align with His Will**: Reflect on your desires and verify they align with God's Word. Proverbs 16:3 states, "Commit to the Lord whatever you do, and he'll establish your plans."

- **Stay Connected**: Surround yourself with believers who uplift and encourage you. Hebrews 10:24-25 emphasizes the importance of community in faith.

- **Act in Faith**: Step out and act on what you feel called to do. 2 Corinthians 5:7 reminds us to walk by faith, not sight.

As you pursue your divine purpose, you'll find clarity in your decisions and strength in your challenges. Trust that God is guiding you every step, illuminating your path, and empowering you to overcome darkness.

You've been designed for a unique purpose—embrace it boldly!

Taking Captivity Captive: The True Meaning

Many believers grapple with the concept of taking captivity captive in the journey of faith, a powerful notion rooted in Scripture. This phrase, drawn from 2 Corinthians 10:5, invites you to recognize your authority in Christ to seize control over thoughts and strongholds that seek to ensnare your spirit.

It's a call to action—to declare that the burdens of doubt, fear, and lies no longer dominate your mind or heart.

Taking captivity captive means understanding that you're not just a passive participant in your spiritual battles. You're equipped with the divine authority to dismantle every argument and high-minded thing that opposes the knowledge of God.

This isn't merely about resisting negativity but actively embracing the truth of who you are in Christ. You're a child of the King, endowed with the power to turn the tide in your life.

As you begin this transformative journey, remember that your weapons aren't of this world. With prayer, faith, and the Word, you can challenge every thought that doesn't align with God's promises.

It's time to rise up! Declare victory over the areas where you feel held captive and witness the chains of oppression break.

Embrace the freedom that comes from taking captivity captive, and let your spirit soar in the light of His truth. You wield the power to redefine your reality, so step boldly into your divine inheritance today!

Submitting and Resisting: The Twofold Battle Plan

Submitting isn't about weakness; it's about surrendering to the all-powerful One. When you yield your will to God, you open the door for His guidance and protection.

Meanwhile, resisting the enemy is equally important. You must stand firm against temptations and lies, wielding the truth as your weapon.

Here are some practical steps to embody this twofold strategy:

- **Pray for strength**: Daily communication with God bolsters your spirit.

- **Meditate on Scripture**: Let His Word be your foundation and shield.

- **Seek accountability**: Surround yourself with believers who uplift and support you.

- **Practice discernment**: Be aware of how the enemy tries to deceive you.

- **Act in faith**: Trust that God's power is at work in you, even when challenges arise.

Overcoming by the Blood and the Testimony

The power of overcoming lies profoundly in the blood of Jesus and your testimony. Revelation 12:11 reminds you that "they overcame him by the blood of the Lamb and by the word of their testimony." This isn't just a concept; it's your weapon in spiritual warfare.

When you acknowledge Jesus' sacrifice, you tap into a divine authority that breaks chains and shatters darkness. The blood of Jesus cleanses you from sin and empowers you to walk in victory. It reminds you that you're not fighting for victory; you're fighting from it.

You proclaim freedom and healing whenever you declare His blood over your life. You're creating a barrier against the enemy's schemes, knowing that no weapon formed against you will prosper (Isaiah 54:17).

But it's not just the blood; your testimony carries weight. Your deliverance, hope, and restoration story is a beacon of light for others. When you share what God has done, you activate faith in yourself and those who hear it.

You're not just recounting events but declaring His faithfulness and power.

Chapter Nine

The Role of Community in Spiritual Warfare

You might underestimate the significance of community in spiritual warfare. Still, it is vital to strengthen your resolve against spiritual adversities. When surrounded by a supportive network, you gain encouragement and accountability that isolation simply can't provide. Collective prayer and shared experiences create a powerful defense. Yet, many still struggle to cultivate such a community effectively. As we explore the intricacies of building these connections, you'll discover strategies to transform your approach to spiritual battles. So, how do you begin to harness this collective power?

Why Spiritual Battles Shouldn't Be Fought Alone

Spiritual battles are intense and often overwhelming, so you must not face them alone. The enemy seeks to isolate you, using fear and doubt to weaken your resolve. In Ecclesiastes 4:9-10, Scripture reminds you, "Two are better than one because they have a good reward for their toil. For if they fall, one will lift up his fellow." When you engage in spiritual warfare, your strength multiplies when you unite with others.

The enemy thrives in darkness and division, but God has designed you for the community. In Galatians 6:2, Paul instructs you to "bear one another's burdens, and so fulfill the law of Christ." This mutual support helps you remain grounded when facing trials. When you share your struggles with fellow believers, you find encouragement and gain wisdom and perspective from their experiences.

Moreover, prayer plays an important role in these battles. James 5:16 says, "The prayer of a righteous person has great power as it's working." When you pray together with others, you invite God's power into your situation, fortifying your spiritual defenses.

Remember that spiritual battles aren't just personal; they affect the community of believers. By standing together, you create a fortified front against the adversary, reflecting the unity that Christ desires for His Body.

Lean on your community, share your burdens, and you'll find strength to face the enemy head-on.

The Power of Shared Faith and Prayer

Shared faith and prayer have immense power, especially when facing spiritual battles. When you gather with others who share your beliefs, you're not just increasing your numbers but amplifying your spiritual strength.

Jesus said in Matthew 18:20, "For where two or three gather in my name, there am I with them." This promise highlights how God's presence is magnified in the community, making your prayers more potent.

When you pray together, you invite God into your struggles. James 5:16 encourages us, "The prayer of a righteous person is powerful and effective."

Your community's collective faith can act like a shield, protecting you from the onslaught of spiritual attacks.

As you lift each other up, you create an environment where God's grace can flow freely.

Moreover, shared faith fosters accountability. When you openly share your struggles, your brothers and sisters in Christ can offer support, encouragement, and even correction when necessary.

This partnership in prayer helps you remain focused and steadfast in your walk with God.

How to Build a Strong Spiritual Support System

Building a strong spiritual support system starts with intentionally connecting with others who share your faith journey. It's crucial to seek out like-minded individuals who can encourage and uplift you as you navigate the challenges of spiritual warfare. Scripture reminds us in Proverbs 27:17, "As iron sharpens iron, so one person sharpens another." This mutual encouragement is important in fortifying your spirit against the enemy's attacks.

Start by joining a community or small group within your church that encourages open discussions about faith and struggles. Don't hesitate to share your experiences and listen to others; vulnerability fosters deeper connections. Regular prayer meetings or Bible studies can also help solidify these relationships, allowing you to grow together in understanding God's word.

Consider finding a mentor or spiritual guide who can offer wisdom and support. Titus 2:3-5 emphasizes the importance of older women teaching younger ones, fostering a sense of accountability and growth. This mentorship can provide guidance and encouragement tailored to your unique situation.

Understanding Spiritual Covering and Leadership

When you grasp the concept of spiritual covering and leadership, you understand the protective and guiding roles that spiritual authority plays in your life. Spiritual covering refers to the divine protection and oversight leaders provide aligned with God's purpose. In Hebrews 13:17, you're reminded to obey and submit to your leaders as they watch over your souls. This relationship isn't merely hierarchical; it's a covenantal bond where leaders shepherd their flock with care and accountability.

Recognizing spiritual leadership helps you navigate the complexities of spiritual warfare. Just as David relied on Samuel's guidance, you, too, can benefit from the wisdom and insight of those appointed to lead. They not only provide counsel but also intercede on your behalf. James 5:16 emphasizes the power of prayer, urging you to confess your sins to one another and pray for each other, allowing the community to strengthen your spiritual armor.

Practically, aligning yourself under spiritual covering means actively engaging with your church community. Attend services, participate in small groups, and seek mentorship. These actions foster deeper connections, allowing you to draw on the encouragement and strength of fellow believers.

Additionally, it's crucial to recognize that spiritual authority isn't about control but love and guidance, reflecting Christ's sacrificial leadership. Embrace the covering provided by your community, and you'll find yourself better equipped to face the battles of the spirit with confidence and clarity.

How to Protect the Spiritually Vulnerable

To protect the spiritually vulnerable, you must first recognize the signs of their fragility. Individuals may struggle with doubt, temptation, or emotional turmoil. Acknowledging these struggles is essential for fostering a supportive healing environment.

The Bible reminds us in Galatians 6:2, "Bear one another's burdens, and so fulfill the law of Christ." By actively engaging with the spiritually vulnerable, you can help them navigate their challenges.

Here are some key ways to protect those who may be feeling spiritually exposed:

- **Listen attentively**: Sometimes, just being there and offering a compassionate ear can make all the difference.

- **Pray fervently**: Commit to praying for them, asking God to shield their hearts and minds from the enemy's attacks.

- **Encourage accountability**: Help them find fellowship with others who can support them in their faith journey.

- **Share scripture**: Remind them of God's promises through His Word, reinforcing their identity in Christ.

Avoiding Spiritual Burnout in Group Battles

While engaging in spiritual battles as a group can be invigorating, it's important to recognize the potential for burnout that often accompanies intense collective efforts. The Bible reminds us in Galatians 6:9, "Let us not become weary in doing good, for at the proper time we'll reap a harvest if we don't give up." This verse underscores the need for perseverance but also implies that weariness is a real threat, particularly in group dynamics.

To avoid spiritual burnout, it's significant to prioritize rest and reflection. Just as Jesus took time away from the crowds (Luke 5:16), you should encourage your group to step back and recharge. Establish regular intervals for rest, prayer, and personal reflection amidst collective activities. This can help maintain spiritual vitality and prevent exhaustion.

Another practical step is cultivating an atmosphere of support and encouragement within your community. Remind each other of your individual callings and the importance of balance, as 1 Corinthians 12 emphasizes the diversity of gifts within the body of Christ. By acknowledging and honoring each member's unique contributions, you can foster a sense of belonging and prevent feelings of isolation.

Lastly, communicate openly about feelings of fatigue or overwhelm. Creating a safe space for vulnerability allows you to address challenges collectively. By intentionally focusing on these areas, you can sustain your group's energy, ensuring you remain effective in the spiritual battles you face together.

Holding Each Other Accountable

Accountability isn't just a good idea; it's a biblical principle that strengthens our spiritual walk and enhances our collective effectiveness in battles. When you hold each other accountable, you're not just checking off a box but engaging in a crucial practice reflecting Christ's love and truth.

Scripture reminds us in Proverbs 27:17, "As iron sharpens iron, so one person sharpens another." This mutual encouragement and challenge is essential for growth.

In your community, you can create an environment where accountability thrives. Consider these key aspects:

- **Encouragement**: Remind each other of God's promises and the purpose behind your battles.

- **Honesty**: Foster an atmosphere where vulnerability is welcomed, allowing for deeper connections.

- **Support**: Be present in each other's struggles, offering prayer and practical help.

- **Challenge**: Don't stop addressing areas that need growth or change, always with love.

By committing to hold each other accountable, you cultivate spiritual resilience. This isn't just about avoiding sin but pushing each other toward holiness and purpose.

As you remind one another of God's truth, your community becomes a fortress against spiritual attacks.

Dealing with Internal Conflict and Disunity

Internal conflict and disunity can be like a hidden enemy, quietly undermining the strength of your community and hindering its mission. Allowing disagreements, bitterness, or unresolved issues to fester creates a rift that makes it harder to stand together against spiritual attacks.

Scripture warns against this in Philippians 2:2-3, urging you to be "like-minded" and value others above you. Unity isn't just a lofty ideal; it's essential for spiritual warfare.

To deal with internal conflict, start by fostering open communication. Encourage members to express their concerns in a safe environment, where resolution is the goal, not winning an argument.

Ephesians 4:15 reminds you to "speak the truth in love," guiding you to approach conflict with grace and compassion. This doesn't mean ignoring the issue; it means addressing it with a heart that seeks reconciliation.

Additionally, prayer is your greatest weapon. When you pray together, you invite God into the situation, allowing Him to soften hearts and guide conversations.

Matthew 18:20 assures you that where two or three gather in His name, He's present. By seeking His wisdom, you'll often find that your perspectives shift, leading to a deeper understanding of each other.

The Role of the Church in Spiritual Warfare

As you confront the challenges of internal conflict and disunity, it's important to recognize the church's significant role in spiritual warfare. The church isn't just a gathering of believers; it's a spiritual battleground where you can find strength, support, and guidance. In the face of spiritual battles, the collective power of the church becomes an essential weapon against the forces of darkness.

Consider these aspects of the church's role:

- **Unity in Christ**: The church fosters a deep sense of belonging, encouraging you to stand firmly against the enemy's schemes (Ephesians 6:11).

- **Prayer Support**: You can join in prayer within the church community, amplifying your spiritual authority (Matthew 18:19-20).

- **Accountability**: The church offers a space for accountability, helping you to bear one another's burdens and grow in faith (Galatians 6:2).

- **Teaching and Discipleship**: Through sound teaching, the church equips you with biblical truths that arm you in spiritual battles (2 Timothy 3:16-17).

In essence, the church is a sanctuary where people can seek wisdom, find encouragement, and engage in collective warfare against spiritual forces.

When you embrace this community, you're not fighting alone; you're part of a larger body, armed with effective and powerful spiritual weapons.

Corporate Worship as a Spiritual Weapon

Corporate worship is a powerful spiritual weapon that unites believers in a collective expression of faith and devotion. When you gather with others, you're not just participating in a routine; you're engaging in a sacred act that can break strongholds and shift spiritual atmospheres.

Scripture underscores this in Matthew 18:20, where Jesus promises, "For where two or three gather in my name, there am I with them." This presence amplifies your collective faith, making your worship a force against spiritual darkness.

Worship is more than a song; it's a declaration of God's sovereignty. As you lift your voice together, you affirm the truth of God's power and character.

Psalm 22:3 reminds us that God inhabits the praises of His people. This divine inhabitation creates a space where spiritual battles are fought and won as we align our hearts and minds with His purposes.

Moreover, corporate worship fosters community and accountability, strengthening one's resolve to stand firm in faith. When people worship together, they share testimonies of God's faithfulness, which can ignite hope and courage in one another.

Ephesians 5:19 encourages believers to "speak to one another with psalms, hymns, and songs from the Spirit," reinforcing that your worship is a mutual edification.

Corporate worship is a profound instrument in spiritual warfare for individual growth and collective victory.

Praying for Each Other: A Shared Shield

Believers' prayers for one another form an essential shield in our daily spiritual battleground. When you lift up your brothers and sisters in prayer, you engage in a profound act of love and solidarity. The Apostle Paul encourages this practice in Ephesians 6:18, urging us to pray in the Spirit on all occasions, highlighting the communal aspect of our spiritual fight.

Your prayers can become the lifeline for those around you, especially during their darkest moments. When you pray for each other, you:

- **Encourage the weary**: Your intercessions can bring hope when others feel overwhelmed.

- **Fortify the weak**: Your spiritual support can strengthen the faith of those struggling.

- **Uphold the lost**: Your prayers can pave the way for the salvation of those in spiritual bondage.

- **Celebrate victories**: Communicating God's faithfulness fosters joy and gratitude.

It's crucial to understand that prayer isn't merely a personal exercise; it's a shared responsibility. Each of you has unique burdens and victories; through prayer, you cultivate a network of divine protection and encouragement.

As you pray, remember James 5:16, which reminds you that the prayer of a righteous person is powerful and effective.

Mentorship and Guiding New Spiritual Warriors

Mentoring new spiritual warriors involves stepping up to guide and empower those just beginning their faith journey. You have a unique opportunity to walk alongside these individuals, helping them navigate the complexities of spiritual warfare.

Your role as a mentor isn't just about imparting knowledge but also about fostering a safe space where questions and doubts can be asked and addressed.

In 2 Timothy 2:2, Paul encourages Timothy to pass on what he's learned to reliable people who will also be qualified to teach others. This idea of multiplication is essential in mentorship. You'll want to equip these new warriors with scriptural understanding and practical tools for engaging in spiritual battles.

Encourage them to immerse themselves in the Word, as Ephesians 6:17 describes the sword of the Spirit as the Word of God. Help them understand how to wield this sword effectively in prayer and daily life.

Share your own experiences, both victories and struggles, to demonstrate that spiritual warfare is a process marked by growth and learning.

Additionally, creates opportunities for them to engage in community, reinforcing the importance of unity in the body of Christ (Philippians 1:27).

By nurturing their spiritual growth through mentorship, you're not just raising warriors; you're building a resilient community that can stand firm against the enemy's schemes.

In doing so, you'll fulfill the Great Commission and foster a legacy of faith that will endure for generations.

Recognizing Spiritual Gifts in the Group

As you guide new spiritual warriors, recognizing the diverse gifts within your group becomes essential for fostering a vibrant community. Each member brings unique abilities that contribute to the collective strength of the body of Christ.

In 1 Corinthians 12:4-7, Paul reminds us, "There are different kinds of gifts, but the same Spirit distributes them. To each one, the manifestation of the Spirit is given for the common good." This verse emphasizes the importance of acknowledging and celebrating these gifts.

To effectively recognize spiritual gifts, encourage open discussions, and create an atmosphere where members feel safe to express their talents. Here are some practical steps to help you identify these gifts:

- **Observe natural inclinations**: Pay attention to what individuals are passionate about and naturally drawn to.

- **Encourage feedback**: Create opportunities for group members to share their observations about each other's strengths.

- **Facilitate assessments**: Utilize spiritual gift inventories to guide individuals in discovering their unique contributions.

- **Pray together**: Seek God's guidance in identifying and affirming each person's gifts, trusting that the Holy Spirit leads the way.

Spiritual Warfare in Family Dynamics

Spiritual warfare profoundly impacts family dynamics, often manifesting in conflicts, misunderstandings, and emotional struggles. You might notice disagreements escalate unexpectedly, or certain patterns of behavior seem to repeat, leaving you feeling trapped. Scripture teaches us that our battle isn't against flesh and blood but against spiritual forces (Ephesians 6:12). Recognizing this truth is essential; it helps you understand that the root of familial strife may be spiritual rather than purely relational.

In your family, you must be vigilant about the words you speak and the attitudes you foster. James 3:5-6 emphasizes how the tongue can cause great destruction, igniting fires that can consume your relationships. Practically, this means approaching conflicts with grace and prayer. When tensions rise, you can pause and ask God for wisdom and understanding, seeking to see the situation from His perspective.

Furthermore, unity in prayer can fortify your family against these spiritual attacks. Matthew 18:19-20 reminds us of the power of collective prayer. Encourage your family to pray together regularly, interceding for each other's struggles, healing wounds, and seeking reconciliation.

Lastly, remember that forgiveness is a powerful weapon in spiritual warfare. Ephesians 4:32 calls you to forgive one another as Christ forgave you. Embracing forgiveness can break chains that bind you to past grievances, allowing your family to move forward in unity and love.

When you recognize the spiritual battles at play, you empower your family to stand firm together.

The Victory of Unity: Winning Battles Together

THE ROLE OF COMMUNITY IN SPIRITUAL WARFARE

Amid spiritual battles, unity becomes a powerful weapon that can transform your family's struggles into victories. When you come together in faith and purpose, you reflect the heart of God, who desires harmony among His children.

The Bible reminds us in Ecclesiastes 4:9-10 that "two are better than one," for they can support each other in times of trouble. This unity allows you to face challenges with renewed strength and resilience.

Consider these four key aspects of unity in spiritual warfare:

- **Shared Prayer**: When you pray together, you invoke God's power and create an environment where His presence can transform situations.

- **Collective Worship**: Worshiping as a family invites the Holy Spirit into your midst, breaking down barriers and uniting your hearts in purpose.

- **Mutual Encouragement**: When one of you falters, the others can uplift and remind one another of God's promises, fostering hope and perseverance.

- **Joint Accountability**: Holding each other accountable strengthens your resolve to resist temptations and works against the schemes of the enemy.

Chapter Ten

After the Battle: Maintaining Spiritual Victory

After a significant spiritual victory, it's easy to let your guard down, but that's often when complacency creeps in. You might question how to maintain that hard-won strength in the face of daily challenges. Engaging in practices like prayer and community support can be essential. Yet, many overlook the importance of reflecting on past battles. Suppose you're ready to explore how to build lasting resilience and prepare for future challenges. In that case, there's much more to uncover about sustaining your spiritual journey.

Living Victoriously: Daily Practices for Protection

As you rise each day, remember that living victoriously isn't just a lofty ideal; it's a commitment to daily practices that invite divine protection into your life. Embrace the truth of Psalm 91:11, which assures you that God commands His angels to guard you in all your ways.

Start your morning praying, seeking His guidance and strength to face the challenges ahead. A few moments in His presence can set the tone for your day.

Next, immerse yourself in His Word. Scripture is a powerful weapon in spiritual warfare, and memorizing verses like Ephesians 6:10-11 can fortify your spirit. As you meditate on these truths, you're not just reading but arming yourself against temptation and doubt.

Cultivating gratitude each day is another practice that invites divine protection. Focusing on blessings shifts your perspective from fear to faith. Consider keeping a gratitude journal to remind yourself of His goodness, especially during trials.

Finally, surround yourself with a community of believers. Fellowship with others not only encourages you but also strengthens your resolve. As iron sharpens iron (Proverbs 27:17), sharing your struggles and victories can help you maintain your spiritual momentum.

Living victoriously isn't about perfection but about intentionality. Establishing these daily practices opens the door to God's protection and guidance, ensuring your spiritual victory remains steadfast.

Guarding Against Complacency After a Win

Victories in your spiritual journey can sometimes lead to a false sense of security, making it easy to let your guard down. You might feel like you've conquered a particular temptation or challenge, but remember that the enemy is always lurking, waiting for the opportune moment to strike. Scripture warns us to be vigilant: "Be sober-minded; be watchful. Your adversary, the devil, prowls around like a roaring lion, seeking someone to devour" (1 Peter 5:8).

Complacency can sneak in when you least expect it, dulling your spiritual senses. After a win, it's vital to stay proactive in your faith. Don't just bask in the glow of your victory; deepen your relationship with God through prayer, worship, and the Word. Maintain the disciplines that fortified you during your struggle.

Consider the Israelites in the Promised Land. After their initial victories, they faced new battles that required constant faith and reliance on God (Joshua 1:9). Your spiritual journey is similar. Each victory equips you for the next challenge but also requires humility and vigilance.

Stay connected to your community of believers. Share your experiences and seek accountability. Acknowledge that victory isn't the end—it's part of a continuous growth journey. Keep your armor on, as Paul instructs in Ephesians 6:11.

Rebuilding Areas Damaged by Spiritual Conflict

Even after experiencing spiritual victories, you may find that certain areas of your life have been battered by conflict. It's vital to recognize that rebuilding is not only possible but essential for your spiritual growth.

Like Nehemiah, who rebuilt the walls of Jerusalem after destruction, you can restore the broken places in your life by relying on God's strength and guidance.

Start by identifying the areas that need healing. Bring these concerns before God in prayer, whether they relate to your relationships, emotional health, or spiritual discipline.

Philippians 4:6-7 reminds us not to be anxious but to present our requests to God, who offers peace beyond understanding.

Next, actively engage in the process of restoration. This might mean seeking counsel from trusted friends, immersing yourself in Scripture, or participating in community worship.

Each step you take lays a brick in the foundation of your renewed life. Ephesians 2:10 tells us that we're God's handiwork, created for good works. Embrace this truth and allow it to motivate you.

Lastly, practice patience. Rebuilding takes time, and you may encounter setbacks.

Remember, God is with you every step of the way. As you lean on His promises and maintain a heart of gratitude, you'll find that these once-damaged areas can become testimonies of His grace and power.

Trust in His ability to restore, and watch as He transforms your struggles into strengths.

Reflecting on Past Battles: Learning and Growing

Battles fought in the spiritual domain often leave us with valuable lessons that can guide our future journeys. Each struggle you've faced has equipped you with insights that deepen your understanding of God's purpose in your life. Remember 2 Corinthians 1:3-4, which reminds us that God comforts us in our troubles so we can comfort others.

Reflecting on past battles allows you to see God's hand at work, even when overwhelmed. As you look back, consider the strategies you employed. What scripture fortified your spirit? What prayers brought you peace? These tools are essential for your ongoing growth.

Each victory and defeat carries a lesson—embrace them. Philippians 3:13-14 encourages you to forget what's behind and strain toward what's ahead, but don't overlook the wisdom gained from your experiences.

You've emerged from each battle transformed, and that reflects your resilience and faith. As you reflect, ask yourself how these lessons can shape your future. Are there areas where you need to apply the wisdom you've gained? Are you ready to share your experiences to uplift others who may be facing similar struggles?

In this journey of learning and growing, let your past battles become stepping stones toward spiritual maturity. Trust that each lesson learned is a part of God's grand design for you, leading you closer to Him and enabling you to stand firm against future challenges. Your growth is a testimony to His faithfulness.

Identifying Residual Strongholds

Examining any residual strongholds that might still linger in your spirit is crucial in the wake of your past struggles. These strongholds can be deceptive, quietly influencing your thoughts and behaviors long after the battle appears won. Scripture reminds us in 2 Corinthians 10:4-5 that "the weapons of our warfare aren't carnal, but mighty through God to the pulling down of strongholds." Identifying these remnants is a significant step toward maintaining your spiritual victory.

Start by reflecting on any recurring patterns in your life that hinder your growth. Are there unexpected thoughts of inadequacy, fear, or bitterness? These can be signs of strongholds still at work. Engage in honest self-examination and prayer, seeking God's guidance to reveal areas where you might still feel defeated.

Consider journaling your thoughts and feelings. Write down any negative beliefs that resurface and counter them with God's truth. For instance, if you often think, "I'm not enough," remind yourself of Philippians 4:13: "I can do all things through Christ who strengthens me."

Moreover, surround yourself with a supportive community. Share your journey with trusted friends or mentors who can help you discern and dismantle these strongholds.

Dealing with Defeat: Rising Up After a Loss

After experiencing a loss, it's easy to feel overwhelmed by disappointment and despair. You might question your strength or even your faith. However, this moment doesn't define you; it's a stepping stone toward greater resilience.

Remember, even the strongest warriors face defeat. In 2 Corinthians 12:9, God reminds you, "My grace is sufficient for you, for my power is made perfect in weakness." Embrace this truth.

Start by acknowledging your feelings. It's okay to grieve a loss but don't let it consume you. Instead, view this as an opportunity for growth. Reflect on what went wrong and what you can learn.

Proverbs 24:16 says, "For though the righteous fall seven times, they rise again." This promise encourages you to rise, no matter how often you stumble.

Surround yourself with a supportive community. Share your struggles, and let others lift you up in prayer and encouragement.

Hebrews 10:24-25 reminds us of the power of fellowship: "And let's consider how we may spur one another on toward love and good deeds."

The Role of Gratitude in Sustaining Victory

Gratitude acts as a powerful anchor that helps you maintain your spiritual victory. When you recognize the blessings in your life, no matter how small, you shift your focus from the battles fought to the victories gained. Philippians 4:6-7 reminds you to present your requests to God with thanksgiving, allowing His peace to guard your heart and mind. This practice cultivates a spirit of thankfulness that strengthens your resilience against future struggles.

In spiritual warfare, the enemy seeks to distract and discourage you. But when you actively choose gratitude, you counteract negativity and doubt. Each time you express thanks, you declare your faith in God's goodness and constant provision. Remember, James 1:17 tells you that every good and perfect gift comes from above. Embracing this truth nurtures an unwavering spirit, reinforcing your victory.

Gratitude also fosters community. When you share your thankfulness with others, you inspire them to recognize their own blessings, creating a ripple effect of positivity. Hebrews 10:24 encourages you to spur one another toward love and good deeds. Your gratitude can uplift those around you, fortifying your spiritual family in their battles.

As you cultivate gratitude, you deepen your relationship with God. It reminds you of His faithfulness and strengthens your resolve to face life's challenges. In this way, gratitude becomes more than a feeling; it's a practice that sustains your spiritual victory, guiding you toward a life of abundance and joy.

How to Maintain a State of Readiness

Recognizing the importance of gratitude empowers you to appreciate your victories and prepares you for the challenges ahead.

When you cultivate a heart of thankfulness, you're more alert and receptive to God's guidance. Staying in a state of readiness means you're not just coasting on past triumphs but actively engaging in the spiritual battle daily.

To maintain this readiness, consider these essential practices:

- **Pray Continuously**: Keep the lines of communication open with God. Philippians 4:6-7 reminds you to present your requests to Him with thanksgiving.

- **Stay in the Word**: Regularly immerse yourself in Scripture. Hebrews 4:12 tells you that the Word is alive and active, equipping you to discern truth from deception.

- **Fellowship with Believers**: Surround yourself with a community that encourages and strengthens your faith. Proverbs 27:17 emphasizes that iron sharpens iron.

- **Practice Self-Examination**: Reflect on your spiritual walk. 2 Corinthians 13:5 urges you to examine yourselves to see if you're in the faith.

Keeping the Enemy Out of Your Life

Guarding your heart and mind against the enemy is crucial in your journey of faith. The enemy prowls like a roaring lion, seeking to devour you (1 Peter 5:8). To keep him out of your life, you must be vigilant and proactive.

Start by anchoring yourself in the Word of God. Scripture is your sword; it cuts through deception and fear. When temptations arise, recall the promises and truths found in the Bible. "It is written" can be your greatest weapon against lies.

Another crucial step is to cultivate a prayerful life. Prayer isn't just talking to God; it's an intimate connection that fortifies your spirit. As you communicate with Him, you gain strength and clarity. Philippians 4:6-7 reminds you to present your anxieties to God, allowing peace to guard your heart and mind.

Furthermore, surround yourself with a supportive community. Fellowship with fellow believers provides encouragement and accountability. As Proverbs 27:17 states, "Iron sharpens iron," reminding us that we grow stronger together.

Stay mindful of what you consume—media, conversations, or environments. Fill your life with positive influences that uplift your spirit and keep negativity at bay. Remember, you have the authority to command peace and reject fear.

How to Prepare for Future Battles

Preparing for future battles in your spiritual journey requires intentionality and readiness. As you move forward, building a strong foundation that can withstand the inevitable challenges is crucial. Remember, you're not alone; God equips you with everything you need to stand firm against spiritual attacks.

Here are some practical steps to prepare:

- **Pray Without Ceasing**: Make prayer a daily habit. It's your direct line to God, who provides strength and wisdom.

- **Immerse Yourself in Scripture**: The Word of God is your sword. Familiarize yourself with verses that speak to your struggles; they'll empower you in times of need.

- **Cultivate a Supportive Community**: Surround yourself with fellow believers who can uplift and encourage you. Together, you'll find strength in unity.

- **Practice Spiritual Discernment**: Be vigilant about your thoughts and influences. Test everything against God's truth to avoid deception.

As you engage in these activities, your faith will deepen. In Ephesians 6:10, Paul reminds us to "be strong in the Lord and in His mighty power."

Preparing for future battles isn't just about being ready for conflict; it's about growing closer to God and building a life anchored in His promises. By taking these steps, you'll withstand the storms and thrive in your spiritual journey, shining His light in a world that desperately needs it.

The Importance of Rest and Spiritual Recovery

Finding moments to rest and recover spiritually is essential for your well-being amidst the hustle and bustle of daily life. Just as Jesus often withdrew to lonely places to pray (Luke 5:16), you, too, need that space to rejuvenate your spirit. When you pause and reflect, you open yourself to God's presence, allowing His peace to fill the void created by life's demands.

Rest isn't just about physical downtime; it's a sacred practice that nourishes your soul. Psalm 23 reminds you, "He makes me lie down in green pastures." This imagery illustrates not only physical rest but emotional and spiritual restoration. God knows your battles and invites you to lay your burdens down, trusting Him to renew your strength.

Engaging in spiritual recovery means intentionally setting aside time for prayer, meditation, and study of the Word. These practices help you reconnect with God, grounding you in His promises. When you immerse yourself in scripture, His truth can reshape your thoughts, fortifying you against future challenges.

Moreover, surrounding yourself with a supportive community fosters healing. Fellowship with others provides encouragement and accountability, reminding you you're not alone in this journey.

Daily Affirmations to Stay Grounded

Everyone can benefit from daily affirmations that anchor them in God's truth and purpose. These affirmations serve as powerful reminders of who you are in Christ and help you stay focused on His promises, especially during challenging times.

When you declare these truths, you're not just speaking words but reinforcing your identity as a beloved child of God.

Consider integrating these affirmations into your daily routine:

- I am fearfully and wonderfully made. (Psalm 139:14)

- God's plans for me are good, to give me hope and a future. (Jeremiah 29:11)

- I am more than a conqueror through Him who loves me. (Romans 8:37)

- I have the mind of Christ and can do all things through Him. (Philippians 2:5; Philippians 4:13)

When you repeat these statements, they become a shield against doubt and negativity. They ground you in the reality of God's love and faithfulness, reminding you that you're equipped for every battle.

Embrace these affirmations as your daily spiritual fuel. Let them permeate your thoughts and actions, transforming how you see yourself and your circumstances.

As you affirm your identity in Christ, you'll find renewed strength and confidence to face each day. Remember, God's truth is your foundation; affirming it daily will help you maintain the spiritual victory He's already won for you.

Staying Spiritually Healthy Amidst Peace

When peace envelops you in the quiet moments of life, it's easy to let your spiritual guard down. You might think that since the battle's over, the fight is done. But remember, even in the calm, the enemy prowls like a roaring lion, seeking whom he may devour (1 Peter 5:8). Staying spiritually healthy during these serene times is essential for your growth and resilience.

Engage daily in prayer and worship, nurturing your relationship with God. James 4:8 reminds you to draw near to Him, and He'll draw near to you. This connection fortifies your spirit and keeps you in tune with His guidance.

Reading and meditating on Scripture is equally important; God's Word is a lamp unto your feet and a light unto your path (Psalm 119:105). It provides wisdom and clarity, ensuring you remain anchored in truth.

Surround yourself with a community that encourages spiritual growth. Fellowship with like-minded believers can help you stay vigilant and accountable. Share your experiences, pray together, and uplift one another, as iron sharpens iron (Proverbs 27:17).

Building a Legacy of Spiritual Victory

While you navigate your spiritual journey, it's crucial to recognize that every decision you make today shapes the legacy you'll leave for future generations. Your choices reflect your faith and the values you instill in those who come after you.

Building a legacy of spiritual victory means living intentionally, drawing on the strength of Scripture and the guidance of the Holy Spirit.

Consider these key elements as you forge your path:

- **Prayerful Discernment**: Seek God's guidance in every decision. James 1:5 reminds us, "If any of you lacks wisdom, let him ask of God."

- **Integrity**: Live authentically, aligning your actions with your beliefs. Proverbs 11:3 states, "The integrity of the upright guides them."

- **Service to Others**: Invest in the lives of those around you. Acts 20:35 encourages us to remember Jesus' words, "It is more blessed to give than to receive."

- **Faithfulness in Trials**: Embrace challenges as opportunities for growth. Romans 5:3-4 teaches that suffering produces perseverance, character, and hope.

As you cultivate these principles, you'll strengthen your own faith and create a powerful legacy that inspires others.

Becoming a Beacon: Helping Others Win Their Battles

Shining your light in the lives of others can transform their battles into victories. Just as Jesus called you to be the world's light (Matthew 5:14), you can guide those around you through their spiritual struggles. When you share your faith and experiences, you inspire others to lean into God's strength, reminding them that they don't have to face their challenges alone.

Consider the power of encouragement. Your words can uplift weary souls, igniting hope in the darkest moments. As 1 Thessalonians 5:11 says, "Encourage one another and build each other up."

Be intentional about reaching out to those who are fighting their own battles. A simple text, a listening ear, or a shared prayer can mean the world to someone in need.

Moreover, sharing your victories can serve as a beacon of hope. When others see how God has worked in your life, they'll realize that their struggles can lead to triumph, too.

2 Corinthians 1:4 emphasizes that God comforts us so we can comfort others. Use your experiences to point them back to the Savior who brings peace amidst chaos.

Ultimately, being a beacon isn't just about your light; it's about reflecting Christ's love. Allow His light to shine through you, and watch as you help others navigate their spiritual warfare.

You can stand firm, united in faith, and emerge victorious.

Conclusion

As we explore spiritual warfare to a close, it's clear that the invisible battles we face are not just theoretical concepts or relics of an ancient worldview. They are deeply interwoven into the fabric of human experience, manifesting in our thoughts, emotions, relationships, and actions. Spiritual warfare is an ongoing reality, challenging us to stand firm in the face of adversity and to develop the inner resilience necessary to withstand assaults on our spirit, mind, and purpose.

Throughout this book, we have explored the hidden dynamics that shape our everyday lives. We have uncovered how spiritual warfare is not limited to dramatic encounters but is often subtle, creeping into our thoughts, whispering lies about who we are, and distorting our perception of reality. This warfare can leave us disoriented, overwhelmed, or disconnected from our true selves and potential. Recognizing these battles for what they are is the first step towards reclaiming our inner strength and authority.

The most crucial takeaway from our journey is that these battles are not ours to fight alone. The weapons and strategies we have discussed—prayer, faith, fasting, scripture, and a clear understanding of identity—are not mere rituals or tools to wield mechanically. They are extensions of a relationship with the divine, empowered by faith and activated through consistent spiritual discipline. Winning in spiritual warfare is less about outward aggression than inward alignment. It's about becoming grounded in truth, nurturing a spirit of peace, and walking in a power that does not depend on our strength but draws from a higher source.

One of the greatest misconceptions about spiritual warfare is that it is an extraordinary occurrence—something reserved for special circumstances or only for those who are spiritually attuned. In reality, regardless of their beliefs or level of spiritual awareness, every person encounters these unseen conflicts. They may not always appear as fierce, supernatural confrontations; they often show up as inner turmoil, toxic patterns, or external opposition that inexplicably hinders progress. But every skirmish, no matter how small, is an opportunity to rise up and declare authority over the forces that seek to bind us in confusion, fear, or despair.

Spiritual warfare calls us to live intentionally, choose whom we will serve daily, and guard what is sacred in our lives—our thoughts, relationships, and purpose. It demands that we stay vigilant, for complacency is one of the enemy's most effective weapons against us. The absence of an active battle does not mean the war is over; it often means the opposition is simply waiting for an opportune time to strike. Maintaining spiritual victory requires continuous watchfulness and an unwavering commitment to living in the light of truth, no matter what shadows may loom.

Another key element is understanding that victory in spiritual warfare is not measured solely by the absence of conflict but by the transformation within us. No matter how painful or draining, every battle can strengthen our resolve, deepen our faith, and refine our character. When we engage rather than retreat, we develop spiritual muscles capable of withstanding future attacks. No matter how small, every victory is a testament to our resilience and a stepping stone to greater victories.

But spiritual warfare is not just a personal battle—it is communal. The strength of a single warrior is amplified when joined by others committed to standing firm together. We are not meant to wage these wars in isolation. A strong spiritual community's support, encouragement, and wisdom can make the difference between victory and defeat. Finding and nurturing these connections is essential. The adversary often targets the isolated, seeking to wear them down and weaken their defenses. In unity, there is strength, and together, we form a bulwark against the onslaught of spiritual opposition.

As we conclude, it's vital to remember that our approach to spiritual warfare should not be rooted in fear or obsession with darkness. Rather, it should be centered on living a life of light, peace, and purpose. It's easy to become consumed with battling evil, constantly looking for signs of attack, and dwelling on what the enemy might be plotting next. But true victory comes from focusing on what empowers us—cultivating love, walking in truth, and standing firm in our identity. The best way to counter darkness is not by fixating on it but by becoming a beacon of light that makes it impossible for darkness to find a foothold.

Moreover, spiritual warfare is not about chasing after power or dominance. It's about restoration and freedom. Every victory should lead us closer to a state of wholeness—within ourselves and our relationships. It's about breaking the chains that bind, uprooting lies, and reclaiming what has been stolen from us: our peace, joy, and sense of purpose. This journey is one of healing and renewal, and every battle won is a step towards the fullness of life we were created to experience.

As we go forward, the challenge is applying what we've learned practically and meaningfully. To engage in spiritual warfare is to embrace a lifestyle of intentionality. It means guarding the gates of your mind against toxic influences, speaking life into hopeless situations, and standing your ground when everything around you urges you to give up. It means recognizing that you are not alone, even when the battle feels overwhelming. There is a power greater than yourself working through you, equipping you with what you need to survive, thrive, and walk in victory.

Remember, the ultimate purpose of spiritual warfare is not just to fight for the sake of fighting. It's to walk in the freedom, purpose, and peace promised. Every skirmish, victory, and setback is part of a larger story—one where you are called to be more than a conqueror, to stand as a testament to the power of faith and the resilience of the human spirit.

So, as you move forward from this book, take courage. Know that every battle, visible or unseen, is an opportunity to become stronger, wiser, and more aligned with your true purpose. Engage boldly, fight with wisdom, and above all, stand firm in the knowledge that you are not defined by the battles you face but by the victories you achieve. Whether in the quiet moments of internal struggle or amid external opposition, remember that you have been equipped for this—called to overcome, to break chains, and to walk in the light of truth. Stay vigilant, stay strong, and always choose to fight for the freedom and peace that are rightfully yours.

Milton Keynes UK
Ingram Content Group UK Ltd.
UKHW040300181024
449757UK00001B/168